About the Author

Paddy Dillon is a prolific outdoor writer with over 30 books to his name, as well as contributions to more than 20 other books. He writes for a number of outdoor magazines and other publications, as well as producing materials for tourism groups and other organisations. He lives on the fringe of the Lake District, and has walked, and written about walking, in every county in England, Scotland, Ireland and Wales. He has led guided walking holidays overseas and has walked in many parts of Europe, as well as Nepal, Tibet and the mountains of Canada and the USA.

While walking his routes, Paddy inputs his notes directly into a palm-top computer every few steps. His descriptions are therefore precise, having been written at the very point at which the reader uses them. He takes all his own photographs and often draws his own maps to illustrate his routes. He has appeared on television, and is a member of the Outdoor Writers' and Photographers' Guild.

Other Cicerone guides written by Paddy include:

Irish Coastal Walks
The Mountains of Ireland
Channel Island Walks
The Isles of Scilly
Walking in the Isle of Arran
Walking the Galloway Hills
The South West Coast Path
Walking in County Durham
Walking the North Pennines
GR20 Corsica: High Level Route

Walking in Madeira
Walking in the Canaries: Vol 1 West
Walking in the Canaries: Vol 2 East
Walking in Malta
North York Moors
The Cleveland Way and Yorkshire Wolds Way
The Irish Coast to Coast Walk
Walking in Mallorca (June Parker, updated Paddy Dillon)

THE GREAT GLEN WAY

by

Paddy Dillon

2 POLICE SQUARE, MILNTHORPE, CUMBRIA LA7 7PY
www.cicerone.co.uk

First edition 2007
ISBN-13: 978 185284 503 2

A catalogue record for this book is available from the British Library.

The spelling of Gaelic placenames in the guide is based on OS and Harvey's maps.

Advice to Readers

Readers are advised that while every effort is taken by the authors to ensure the accuracy of this guidebook, changes can occur which may affect the contents. It is advisable to check locally on transport, accommodation, shops, and so on, but even rights of way can be altered.

The publisher would welcome notes of any such changes.

Front cover: The Caledonian Canal links with the southern part of Loch Ness close to the village of Fort Augustus (Day 3 N–S / Day 4 S–N)

CONTENTS

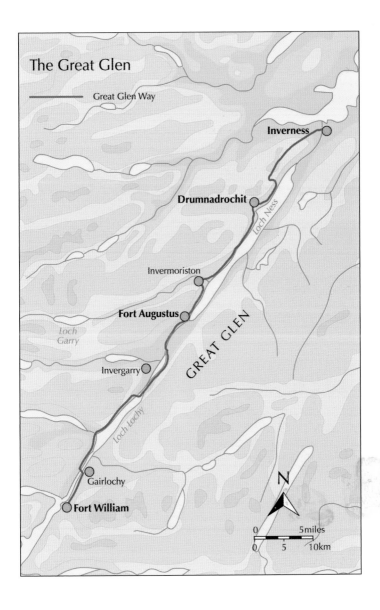

The Great Glen

Great Glen Way

Inverness

Drumnadrochit

Loch Ness

Invermoriston

Fort Augustus

GREAT GLEN

Loch Garry

Invergarry

Loch Lochy

Gairlochy

Fort William

N

0   5 miles
0   5   10km

Boats moored on the Caledonian Canal at Laggan, not far from Loch Lochy Youth Hostel and North Laggan (Day 2 S–N / Day 5 N–S).

INTRODUCTION

The Great Glen is a remarkable geographic feature, running ruler-straight from coast to coast through the Scottish Highlands. Loch Ness, Loch Lochy and little Loch Oich are neatly arranged through the glen, while steep and forested slopes rise towards splendid mountains to north and south. Man has not missed the opportunity to run a road through this low-lying glen, and the Caledonian Canal was cut through the glen linking its three lochs with the coast. Walkers are now blessed with the provision of a waymarked trail through the glen, running for 117 kilometres (73 miles) from Fort

The standard waymark for all Scottish long distance walking routes is a 'thistle' with directional arrows.

William to Inverness via Fort Augustus. It was officially opened on 30th April 2002 by Prince Andrew, Earl of Inverness. As a low-lying trail, most walkers could complete it at most times of the year, and there is always ready access to accommodation, food, drink and transport services.

The Great Glen Way provides an easy and scenic route through the Highlands, where walkers can admire the rugged mountains without having to climb them. Much of the route runs concurrent with the Great Glen Mountain Bike Trail, but there are several paths that are only for the use of walkers. Take the time to delve into the long and turbulent history of clan rivalry, strife and warfare. Marvel at the engineering associated with military roads, railway lines and the Caledonian Canal. Keep an eye peeled for a glimpse of the celebrated Loch Ness Monster!

GEOLOGY

If the Great Glen has a fault, then it is the Great Glen Fault! Even a casual glance at a map of Scotland reveals the true scale and extent of the Great Glen; a suspiciously ruler-straight trench running north-east to south-west. The underlying cause is geological, as the Great Glen lies on a major fault line. The fault has an incredibly long history, having become active some 400 million years ago. However, the rocks either side of it are considerably older! The fault is termed a 'wrench fault' and the land on either side has been displaced over a staggering 105 kilometres (65 miles) or more. It is an interesting exercise to trace out a map of Scotland, cut with scissors along the Great Glen, then slide the northern half of the map that distance along the line of the fault. All other geological events being equal, that is what Scotland would look like if the Great Glen Fault had never existed!

Geologists have studied the granite bedrock near the villages of Foyers and Strontian, and although there is some dispute, many have concluded that they are essentially the same. However, these ancient granite emplacements lie on opposite sides of the Great Glen far distant from each other, ripped apart by the Great Glen Fault. The line of the fault is still considered active and it can give an occasional slight judder. Slight shock waves have been known to disturb the surfaces of the lochs, and structural damage has been caused in the past in Inverness. Earthquakes include one in 1816 that was felt throughout Scotland, with other notable events recorded in 1888, 1890 and 1901.

Weather conditions can change rapidly, but the Great Glen Way is essentially a low-level walking route, Loch Oich (Day 3 S–N / Day 4 N–S).

The power unleashed during such incredible movements has crushed an enormous band of rock along both sides of the fault. In places, the crushed and weakened rock can be up to 1.5km (1 mile) broad. During the Ice Ages, when huge glaciers formed in the Highlands, the already weakened line of the Great Glen Fault was deepened considerably by the inexorable power of slowly moving glaciers. The broken rock along the line of the fault was more easily ground, crushed and moved than the solid rock of the mountains alongside, so that the Great Glen was carved considerably deeper than other Highland glens. As a result, low-lying hollows flooded when the ice melted, some 10,000 years ago, and have remained flooded ever since. The highest part of the Great Glen is occupied by the relatively shallow Loch Oich, while heading south-west, Loch Lochy is broader and deeper. Heading north-east, Loch Ness is broader and deeper, again, with its lowest levels being around 180m (600ft) below sea level!

BRIEF HISTORY

The history of the Scottish Highlands often seems remote from the history of the Lowlands. The Highlands were often inhabited by people with distinct cultural differences to those found further south. The Romans pushed into the area, but retreated. The Picts held sway for centuries, but were later eclipsed by the 'Scots',

who came from Ireland. A thriving Gaelic civilisation existed in the Highlands throughout several centuries when Scottish history was wrought largely in terms of strife and warfare against England. Cromwellian troops subdued the Highlands in the 17th century, but there were notable rebellions in the 18th century, before the region was finally 'tamed'. The timeline history in the appendix to this guidebook focuses more on events in the Great Glen and the Highlands, and less on events in Edinburgh or on the Scots/English border.

THE CALEDONIAN CANAL

The low-lying Great Glen, with its three convenient lochs, was considered an ideal location for a coast-to-coast canal as early as 1726. However, Scotland was quickly embroiled in strife, and no further plans were considered until well after the Jacobite rising of 1745. Following a number of surveys, a serious proposal was put forward in 1802, and Thomas Telford was engaged to design and oversee construction. Although the Caledonian Canal is said to measure 96.5 kilometres (60 miles), only 35.5 kilometres (22 miles) is actually man-made. The cut sections of the canal were engineered between 1803 and 1822; the first government-funded transport project in Britain. There are four aqueducts, ten bridges and 29 locks.

11

The Caledonian Canal seen here at Gairlochy is a remarkable coast-to-coast canal routed straight through the Great Glen (Day 1 S–N / Day 6 N–S).

The Caledonian Canal was created primarily to allow safe passage for naval vessels at the time of the Napoleonic Wars, but was not really used by the military until the Great War. As a through route for trading vessels, allowing a short cut through Scotland, the canal boosted the local economy. Large commercial craft still use the canal, but these days most vessels are leisure craft, plying through some of the most splendid canal-side scenery anywhere in the world. As the locks are operated by employees of British Waterways Scotland, they have set daily operating hours. Also, as there is a 5-knot speed limit on the canal, even the most determined cruisers should allow a minimum of 14 hours sailing, spread over two and a half days, to negotiate the Caledonian Canal.

Those with an interest in cruising through the Great Glen should contact: Caledonian Canal Office, Seaport Marina, Muirtown Wharf, Inverness, IV3 5LE (☎01463-233140).

ANIMALS AND PLANTS

The Great Glen Way starts and finishes on tidal inlets, and often runs within sight of broad lochs, stretches of canals and rivers. However, the glen is flanked by steep and rugged slopes, well forested for the most part, although there is some farmland on the floor of the glen. As there are a variety of wildlife habitats, there is plenty for an observant walker to see along the way.

The largest wild mammals are of course red deer, though there are also smaller sika deer and hybrids of both species. Deer are generally stalked from mid-August to mid-October, and anyone leaving the course of the Great Glen Way and heading for more remote places should be aware of this. The best places to observe deer are around the margins of woodland and forest at dawn and dusk, though they can be seen anywhere throughout the day. During the autumn, or 'rutting' season, red deer stags emit a deep-throated call known as 'belling', while sika deer make more of a whistling sound. The woodlands and forests of the Great Glen are strongholds of the red squirrel and pine marten, both in serious decline in many parts of Britain.

Scotland's native woodlands have been decimated over the past couple of thousand years. The most notable tree is the Scots pine, which is Britain's only native pine, and once formed extensive Caledonian forests. The Forestry Commission is playing a leading part in re-establishing this species. When growing close together, Scots pines form tall and straight trunks, with branches that die off, leaving a green crown. In isolation, the lower limbs of a Scots pine will often grow almost as thick as the main trunk, and are often bent into grotesque forms. Oak, birch, hazel, ash and rowan will be seen from time

13

to time, but with so much land planted with imported conifers, deciduous woodlands are of limited extent. Beech trees flourish in many places, though these were introduced to the Great Glen.

While seabirds will doubtless be noticed at either end of the Great Glen, they are also found at many points along the way, using the low-lying, loch-filled corridor as they cross from coast to coast. Gulls, geese, ducks and even cormorants or shearwaters could be spotted at any point where they are attracted by water. Also look out for grey herons as they patiently wait for fish, or more rarely, ospreys as they dive dramatically for a catch. Other birds of prey include golden eagles, buzzards, kestrels and merlins, while owls are also present. All seek small mammals such as mice and voles. Speak to a fisherman if you want to know what is in the lochs and waterways, or look out for salmon as they work their way inland to spawn late in the summer.

The growing season at such northerly latitudes is short, but summer days are very long and the abundance of water is an advantage for many species. While flowering plants may start to bloom late, they can continue to bloom long after the same species further south have set seed and died back. Few things compare with the sight of rampant flowery watersides in early summer, or the purple heather on moorland slopes later in the summer. Ling

heather is of course dominant, but there is plenty of bell heather too. While red grouse can be spotted on heather moorlands, the rarer black grouse is only likely to be spotted on the Dochfour Estate near Inverness. In the autumn months, when the deciduous trees turn russet and gold, the scenery through the Great Glen can be astonishingly colourful.

THE LOCH NESS MONSTER

The year was AD565 and a follower of St Columba was swimming across Loch Ness to get a boat for his master. Suddenly, 'with a great roar and open mouth', a monster rose from the loch and bore down on the swimmer. St Columba swiftly intervened, commanding the monster, 'think not to go further, nor touch thou that man'. The monster sank back into the loch and caused barely a ripple of concern throughout succeeding centuries.

The whole world has seen the grainy black and white image that seems to show a tapering neck and head above the waters of Loch Ness. It is generally referred to as the 'surgeon's photograph' and was taken by the Harley Street consultant R. K. Wilson in 1934. Since that time, there have been several 'sightings' of 'Nessie', as well as a number of amateur and professional 'hunts' around and within Loch Ness. Some photographs are easily dismissed as fakes, while others have enjoyed a

Some people believe the Loch Ness 'monster', seen here at Drumnadrochit, to be an ancient plesiosaur, marooned in the deep water (Day 5 S–N / Day 1 N–S).

period of notoriety before an admission of foul play is made. Vast sums of money have been sunk into the dark and murky depths of the loch, and while some might say that there has been little return for the investment, it has been great for tourism. One only needs to observe the coaches rumbling alongside the loch, or the cruisers that take trippers out onto the water, to say nothing of those who eagerly scan the surface for sight of something … anything.

There may or may not be a Loch Ness Monster, and in the absence of evidence one way or the other, visitors are free to believe what they wish. Two things are true: first, 'Nessie' does draw a lot of visitors to the area. Second, human beings have a proven capacity to believe almost anything, no matter how bizarre, and

scientific proof is not always necessary. Those who are wavering in their belief are amply catered for at Drumnadrochit, where the Original Loch Ness Monster Visitor Centre and the Official Loch Ness Exhibition Centre clamour for attention. Shops throughout the Great Glen sell a variety of 'monsters', some smooth and sinuous, others plump and furry, some ferocious, but most of them happy and smiling, wearing kilts or playing bagpipes. You pay your money and you make your choice!

TRAVEL TO THE GREAT GLEN

Air
The nearest airport to the Great Glen is Inverness Airport (☎01463-232471, **www.invernessairport.com**).

There are direct flights to Inverness from major British airports such as Heathrow, Gatwick, Birmingham, Manchester, Glasgow and Edinburgh. The only real budget operator is Easyjet, **www.easyjet.com**, flying direct from Luton to Inverness. Direct flights to Inverness from around Europe are currently limited to those from Stockholm, Mallorca, Ibiza and Lanzarote. Rapson's Highland Country buses and local taxis operate from the airport into the centre of Inverness, which is very handy for the northern terminus of the Great Glen Way, or for onward bus services to Fort William. A much greater number of flights operate to Glasgow and Edinburgh, with most budget flights landing at Prestwick. All three airports have good public transport links to the cities for onward transport to the Great Glen by train or bus.

Rail

Virgin Trains, **www.virgintrains.co.uk**, operate backbone rail services through Britain to Glasgow, Edinburgh and Aberdeen. First ScotRail, **www.firstgroup.com/scotrail**, provides onward rail travel from Glasgow to Fort William, or from Edinburgh and Aberdeen to Inverness. Walkers travelling from continental Europe can take advantage of combined Eurostar and Caledonian Sleeper services from Lille, Paris or Brussels in order to reach Fort William or Inverness refreshed and ready to start walking.

Coach

National Express coaches, **www.nationalexpress.co.uk**, from all over England and Wales converge on Glasgow and Edinburgh to link with Scottish Citylink coaches, **www.citylink.co.uk**, to Fort William and Inverness. Walkers from around Europe can book coach travel through Eurolines, **www.eurolines.com**, that will include onward travel with National Express and Scottish Citylink coach services.

Car

Use the M6 and A74/M74 to travel north to Glasgow, then skirt the city on the M8 to follow the A82 north to Fort William. The A82 runs roughly parallel to the celebrated West Highland Way. Alternatively, use the A1 to reach Edinburgh and cross the Forth Road Bridge, then follow the M90 and A9 north to Inverness. Walkers who require safe parking for a week could have problems. However, parking is available at Invergarry for those who use the baggage transfer services offered by Great Glen Travel (☎01809-501222, **www.greatglentravel.com**).

TRAVEL THROUGH THE GREAT GLEN

Bus

Rapson's Highland Country buses, **www.rapsons.com**, operate many services in and around the Great Glen.

There are comprehensive town services around Fort William and Inverness, as well as a few buses through the Great Glen each day. Most of the buses through the Great Glen are operated by Scottish Citylink, **www.citylink.co.uk**. All bus services through the glen follow the main A82 road, serving Fort William, Spean Bridge, Laggan, Invergarry, Aberchalder, Fort Augustus, Invermoriston, Alltsigh, Drumnadrochit and Inverness. On average, buses operate every two hours, and the full journey through the Great Glen takes two hours. With a careful study of current bus timetables, walkers could operate from a single base in the Great Glen, commuting to and from sections of the route each day. However, as the A82 is a busy road, drivers may insist that you use only the recognised bus stops, and they may not be able to stop at all on some parts of the road.

Car

The A82 is the main road through the Great Glen from Fort William to Inverness. Anyone accompanied by a back-up vehicle will find access to the Great Glen Way at several points, including Fort William, Inverlochy, Caol, Corpach, Banavie, Gairlochy, Achnacarry, Clunes, Laggan, Invergarry, Aberchalder, Fort Augustus, Allt na Criche, Invermoriston, Alltsigh, Balbeg, Drumnadrochit, Abriachan Forest, Ladycairn, Blackfold and Inverness.

Ferry

The Loch Ness Express offers a wonderful opportunity to travel halfway through the Great Glen by ferry. The 36-seater vessel generally operates from the beginning of May until the end of December. It runs from Dochgarroch, near Inverness, to Fort Augustus. There are two return journeys per day from May to October, then one return journey per day in November and December. There are free shuttle buses to the ferry berth at Dochgarroch from the Tourist Information Centre in Inverness. Freephone 0800-3286426 or visit **www.lochnessexpress.com** for details.

TRAVELINE SCOTLAND

Any public transport service, anywhere in Scotland, whether it is by bus, train or ferry, can be checked or confirmed simply by contacting Traveline Scotland (☎0870-6082608, website **www.travelinescotland.com**).

FAMILIARISATION WITH THE GREAT GLEN

Walkers can easily familiarise themselves with the Great Glen by driving along the main A82 road. The budget method of familiarisation simply involves catching a bus between Fort William and Inverness, watching the scenery passing by for two hours. Those with more time at their disposal, not to mention money, could book on one of the 'floating

17

hotel' barges, such as the 'Scottish Highlander', and watch the scenery for the best part of a week from the Caledonian Canal and the broad lochs along the way.

ACCOMMODATION

A comprehensive accommodation booklet, updated each year and free of charge, is available from the Great Glen Way Rangers or Tourist Information Centres along the Great Glen Way. It is packed with all sorts of other information about the current range of facilities along the route, and should be obtained and carefully consulted well in advance of walking the route. This guidebook indicates where accommodation is available, but the Great Glen Way Accommodation and Services Guide gives you the full contact details.

It is essential to book accommodation well in advance if you plan to walk during the peak summer season, as lodgings are very sparse in some places. If an address is some distance off-route, it may be possible to arrange to be collected in the evening and dropped off the following morning, but ask about this when making a booking. Accommodation can be booked while on the move, either through Tourist Information Centres along the way or through Visit Scotland by telephone. With Visit Scotland, you can pay in advance by credit card, which may not be an option with individual establishments.

If calling from within the UK, phone 0845-2255121. If calling from outside the UK, phone +44-1506-832121. Contact made by this method will ensure that you are placed in accommodation listed with the tourist board, but there are also a number of unlisted addresses that will become apparent along the way.

Always remember that when you make a booking with an accommodation provider, a contract exists between you. If you fail to show, then you could lose any deposit paid, or even the full amount if already paid. Also, failure to show could cause concern for your well-being, and the rescue services might be alerted unnecessarily. If you think you will not be able to take up accommodation you have booked, please contact the provider and tell them.

Camping

While there are no campsites actually on the course of the Great Glen Way, some can be reached by walking a short distance off-route. Campsites can be found at or near Glen Nevis, Gairlochy, Invergarry, Fort Augustus, Invermoriston, Drumnadrochit, Abriachan Forest and Inverness. Wild camping is possible in many places, subject to the provisions of the Land Reform (Scotland) Act 2003. Those who choose to camp wild for an occasional night should do so discreetly, well away from habitations, and keep their pitches scrupulously clean.

There are plenty of lodgings through the Great Glen, but they are unevenly spread and may lie off-route. Aberchalder (Day 3 S–N / Day 4 N–S)

19

An idyllic loch-shore pitch beside Loch Lochy (Day 2 S–N / Day 5 N–S), but is it legal to camp in the wilds? Refer to the Scottish Outdoor Access Code to find out.

Hostelling

There are four Scottish Youth Hostel Association (SYHA) (www.syha.org.uk) properties along the course of the Great Glen Way, which are insufficient to cover the distance. Walkers who wish to use the hostels may have to consider using bus services to reach them from certain points along the way. The hostels are located at Glen Nevis, near Fort William; Loch Lochy, at Laggan; Loch Ness, at Alltsigh; and Inverness, in the city centre. Bunkhouse and independent hostel accommodation is available at Corpach, Gairlochy, Invergarry, Fort Augustus and Inverness, which should help to fill some of the gaps in the chain of SYHA hostels.

Hotels and bed and breakfast

There are plenty of bed and breakfast establishments through the Great Glen, as well as hotels in some places, offering a higher degree of comfort and privacy, at a higher price. If evening meals or packed lunches are required, please tell your accommodation provider when making a booking, since these may be difficult to organise at short notice. Some providers, while unable to offer meals, may be willing to take walkers to nearby restaurants for a meal, but again, ask about this when booking.

FOOD AND DRINK

There are plenty of places offering food and drink along the course of the Great Glen Way, but they are very unevenly distributed. In places such as Fort William, Fort Augustus, Drumnadrochit and Inverness, there are plenty of shops, bars, restaurants, cafés and take-aways available. In places such as Invermoriston there are only a couple of restaurants, while around Laggan and Gairlochy, the choice is even more limited, and when places are closed, it might be necessary to catch a bus elsewhere if you are not carrying food. Shops and places offering food and drink are mentioned throughout this guidebook, and if there are lengthy stretches where nothing is mentioned, then assume that nothing is available and be sure to carry some kind of drink and snack with you to cover the distance.

MONEY

Most accommodation and food providers along the Great Glen Way deal only in cash, though some will take cheques or credit cards. There are a few ATMs along the way, at Fort

Facilities along the Great Glen Way include offers of accommodation, food, drink, shops, banks, etc.

William, Spean Bridge, Fort Augustus, Drumnadrochit and Inverness, but bear in mind that some of these may be inside shops and may not be available on a 24-hour basis. Those who have never visited Scotland before will find that banknotes are issued by the Bank of Scotland, Royal Bank of Scotland and Clydesdale Bank, and these are used alongside Bank of England notes, so your wallet may often contain quite a variety of banknotes. Study them carefully if you are unfamiliar with them. Scottish banknotes are legal tender throughout Britain, though the further you travel from Scotland, the more difficult it can be to spend them, though banks are always willing to change them.

TOURIST INFORMATION CENTRES

There are a handful of Tourist Information Centres along the Great Glen Way. Contact them for details of local facilities, including transport and accommodation, food and drink, and the opening times, locations and charges for nearby attractions. Some will be able to book accommodation for you, or at least point you in the direction of lodgings, and many of them sell useful maps and background literature, as well as gifts and souvenirs.

Fort William – TIC, Cameron Square, Fort William, PH33 6AJ, ☎01397-703781, email fortwilliam@host.co.uk

Spean Bridge – Kingdom of Scotland
  Visitor Centre, Spean Bridge,
  PH34 4EP, ☎01397-712999,
  email treasures@kingdomofscot-
  land.co.uk
Glengarry Visitor Centre – Invergarry,
  PH35 4HJ, ☎01809-501424
Fort Augustus – TIC, Car Park, Fort
  Augustus, PH32 4DD,
  ☎01320-366367,
  email fortaugustus@host.co.uk
Drumnadrochit – TIC, The Village
  Car Park, Drunmadrochit, IV63
  6TX, ☎01456-459050, email
  drumnadrochit@host.co.uk
Inverness – TIC, Castle Wynd,
  Inverness, IV2 3BJ,
  ☎01463-234353,
  email inverness@host.co.uk

MAPS OF THE ROUTE

The Ordnance Survey covers the Great
Glen Way on three Landranger maps at
a scale of 1:50,000. The sheet numbers
are 26, 34 and 41. Linear extracts from
these maps are reproduced throughout
this guidebook, with the route high-
lighted. Three Ordnance Survey
Explorer maps cover the route at a scale
of 1:25,000, and the sheet numbers
are 392, 400 and 416
(www.ordnancesurvey.co.uk). Harvey
produce a specific detailed map of the
Great Glen Way Long Distance
Route at a scale of 1:40,000
(www.harveymaps.co.uk). The relevant
maps to use on each day's walk are
mentioned throughout this guidebook.

Route symbols on OS maps extracts

〰	route
〰	alternative route/detour
🚶	start point
🚶	finish point
⬆N	northbound route
⬇S	southbound route

For OS symbols key see OS maps

WHEN TO WALK

Most walkers will choose to trek
through the Great Glen in the peak
summer period. This can be a
splendid time, weather-wise, with as
much as 18 hours of good daylight.
However, it is also a busy time and
there can be a lot of pressure on
accommodation and services along
the way. However, all services will
certainly be in full swing and are there
to be used. Those who walk in spring
or early summer will be able to enjoy
the added colour of wild flowers
along the way, while those who walk
in late summer should be able to
catch the purple heather at its
blooming best.

Summer is also the peak breeding
season for the voracious 'midge'; a
tiny mosquito that can cause distress-
ingly itchy bites. Midges favour still
conditions in the mornings and
evenings, and are unlikely to be a
problem in the middle of sunny,

windy or rainy days. Most walkers move at a pace that outwits the midge, denying it a chance to land on the skin, but at every resting point, they seize the opportunity to feed on your blood. There are a number of repellants on the market, which meet with mixed reviews from users, but the less skin that is exposed, the less skin will be bitten.

Autumn brings its own delights, as the days are often cool and ideal for walking, and most services are still operating, though with less pressure on them. As the deciduous trees and bracken-clad slopes turn russet and golden, the scenery can be breath-taking. However, the weather can be wet, windy and misty at times, and some parts may become wet and muddy.

Winter walking is possible, since the low-lying Great Glen is often free of snow even when there are deep drifts elsewhere. A thin covering of snow will not be a problem, but care should always be taken on icy slopes. Deep drifts, though short-lived, can make walking very difficult. Camping might not be the best option in the winter months, unless walkers are particularly hardy and possess the right gear for it. The chance to finish the day by a blazing fire in cosy lodgings has much more appeal, but bear in mind that not all the accommodation will be open throughout the winter months. Also note that midwinter daylight hours are very short; maybe as little as six hours!

DAILY SCHEDULE

The Great Glen Way can easily be walked within a week, and most walkers will aim to complete the route in five or six days. The daily stages are likely to be uneven, and while some walkers will happily walk an occasional long day, others would split a long day into two shorter days.

The first thing to decide is whether to walk from Fort William to Inverness, south to north, or Inverness to Fort William, north to south. From a practical point of view, walking from Fort William to Inverness means that you are more likely to have the sun behind you, with the prevailing wind, and hence the weather, heading in your direction. Rainfall also tends to decrease markedly in this direction. However, the route becomes progressively more difficult, with the higher and more remote stretches coming towards the end.

Those who choose to walk from Inverness to Fort William can cover the hilly parts first, but should bear in mind that if bad weather is coming from the south-west, as it usually does, then they may be walking directly into it. The route does become easier and lower on the way towards Fort William, but the weather may become progressively wetter. Many walkers who have covered the route both ways are convinced that the scenery is better when walking north to south, or at least, they are more aware of it.

This guidebook describes the Great Glen Way in both directions, and given the connection with the West Highland Way at Fort William, there is no reason why both trails shouldn't be walked together in one long journey between Glasgow and Inverness, or vice versa. Many walkers also find themselves drawn to climb Ben Nevis while based at Fort William.

SCOTTISH OUTDOOR ACCESS CODE

The Land Reform (Scotland) Act 2003 has established a statutory right of access to land and inland waters for outdoor recreation. The *Scottish Outdoor Access Code* gives guidance on your responsibilities when exercising access rights. The Act sets out where and when access rights apply. The Code defines how access rights should be exercised. The *Scottish Outdoor Access Code* is available on leaflets that can be obtained from Scottish Natural Heritage, tourist information centres and local government offices, as well as on the website **www.outdooraccess-scotland.com**.

The Great Glen Way is a waymarked trail so there are no access issues along the route. If you explore around the route, then normal provisions of the Scottish Outdoor Access Code need to be followed. You have a right of responsible access, subject to the code.

The following is a summary of the Code:

- Respect the interests of other people: be considerate, respect privacy and livelihoods, and the needs of those enjoying the outdoors.
- Care for the environment: look after the places you visit and enjoy. Care for wildlife and historic sites.
- Take responsibility for your own actions: the outdoors cannot be made risk-free for people exercising access rights; land managers should act with care for people's safety.

The responsibility of recreational countryside users can be summarised as follows:

- Take responsibility for your own actions: the outdoors is a great place to enjoy, but it is also a working environment and has many natural hazards. Make sure you are aware of these and act safely, follow any reasonable advice and respect the needs of other people enjoying or working in the outdoors.
- Respect people's privacy and peace of mind: privacy is important for everyone. Avoid causing alarm to people, especially at night, by keeping a reasonable distance from houses and gardens, or by using paths or tracks.
- Help land managers and others to work safely and effectively: keep a safe distance from any

work and watch for signs that tell you dangerous activities are being carried out, such as tree felling or crop spraying. Do not hinder land management operations and follow advice from land managers. Respect requests for reasonable limitations on when and where you can go.

- Care for the environment: follow any reasonable advice or information, take your litter home, treat places with care and leave them as you find them. Don't recklessly disturb or damage wildlife or historic places.
- Keep your dog under proper control: it is very important that it does not worry livestock or alarm others. Don't let it into fields with calves and lambs, and keep it on a short lead when in a field with other animals. Do not allow it to disturb nesting birds. Remove and carefully dispose of dog dirt.
- Take extra care if you are organising an event or running a business and ask the landowner's advice. Check the full version of the Code for further details about your responsibilities.

RESCUE SERVICES

The Great Glen Way is essentially a low-level route and is usually close to roads and habitations, so there are few dangers. Obviously, common sense dictates that walkers should take care next to canals, rivers and lochs, as well as when crossing or following roads. The waymarking system is good, so route-finding difficulties are unlikely. If a marker has not been seen for some time, you may be off-route and it might be a good idea to retrace your steps. If the emergency services are needed at any point, police, ambulance, fire, mountain rescue and coastguard are all alerted by dialling 999 (or the European emergency number of 112). Be ready to give full details of the emergency, and give your phone number so that the emergency services can keep in touch. Members of the public cannot request direct helicopter assistance; their call-out and use will be determined by the emergency services based on the information you provide. A small first-aid kit should be carried to deal with any minor cuts, grazes and injuries along the way. Aim to be self-sufficient for each day by carrying food and drink in your pack.

GREAT GLEN WAY RANGERS

Should any problems be noticed along the course of the Great Glen Way, there is a team of rangers ready to address them. Contact the Great Glen Way Rangers, Auchterawe, Fort Augustus, Inverness-shire, PH32 4BT, ☎01320-366633, email greatglenway@highland.gov.uk. The official Great Glen Way website is **www.greatglenway.com**.

THE GREAT GLEN WAY – SOUTH TO NORTH

Looking across the Caledonian Canal, in a cutting at North Laggan, towards Meall na Teanga (Day 3 South to North).

FORT WILLIAM

While the Highlands and islands of Scotland can boast a long and proud Pictish and Gaelic history, the bustling town of Fort William is a relatively new development. There was little in the way of settlement up to the 17th century, until a wooden fort was built by General Monck in 1654, on the orders of Oliver Cromwell. A stone fort replaced it in 1690, built by General Mackay, who named it Fort William in honour of William of Orange. The town that grew alongside the fort was named Maryburgh. The Gaelic name for the town has always been An Ghearasdan, which means The Garrison. The Jacobites mounted a siege in 1746, but the fort stood fast. Maryburgh was rebuilt with wood in 1750, so that it could be quickly burnt and destroyed in the event of a further siege, rather than fall into enemy hands.

A pleasant green space can be found just off the High Street in Fort William near the start of the walk.

Fort William prospered following the arrival of the West Highland Railway Company in 1889, allowing early tourists to reach the Highlands more easily. However, this led to most of the stone fort being destroyed. Most of the buildings seen around town are 19th and 20th century, and the West Highland Museum on Cameron Square is worth a visit (☎01397-702169). The Tourist Information Centre is also on Cameron Square (☎01397-703781).

Facilities around Fort William include plenty of accommodation options, with a campsite and youth hostel available in nearby Glen Nevis. There are banks with ATMs, a post office, toilets, plenty of pubs, restaurants, cafés and take-aways. There are plenty of shops too, including several gift shops and outdoor equipment shops. Fort William has recently re-branded itself as the 'Outdoor Capital of the UK', and after a quick exploration of the town, most active visitors will be keen to head for the hills, or set off along walking routes such as the West Highland Way or Great Glen Way.

Fort William is served by good road and rail links, while town services are operated by Highland Country Buses (☎01397-702373, **www.rapsons.com**).

The original gateway to the garrison at Fort William was rebuilt at the entrance to a cemetery on Belford Road.

DAY 1

Fort William to Gairlochy

Start	Railway Station, Fort William – grid ref 105742
Finish	Gairlochy Bottom Lock – grid ref 176842
Distance	17km (10.5 miles)
Total Ascent	40m (130ft)
Maps	OS Landranger 41, OS Explorers 392 & 400, Harvey Great Glen Way
Terrain	Low-level paths, tracks and roads near the coast, followed by a long, clear canal-side track.
Refreshments	Plenty of bars, restaurants, cafés and take-aways around Fort William. Shops and take-aways at Caol. Shops and bars at Corpach. Bar and restaurant at Banavie. Tearoom at Gairlochy.
Public Transport	Rapson's Highland Country buses run all the town services around Fort William, and also serve Caol, Corpach and Banavie. There are also trains between Fort William, Banavie, Caol and Corpach, as well as between Spean Bridge and Fort William. There is a schooldays-only bus service linking Fort William, Gairlochy, and Spean Bridge.

The Great Glen Way starts near the coast in the busy Highland town of Fort William, in the shadow of Britain's highest mountain. This is an easy day's walk, with a simple riverside path and a short coastal path giving way to a clear and obvious canal-side track. There is very little climbing, and most of that comes in very short stages alongside canal locks. Most of the day's walk is actually on a long and narrow 'island', flanked on one side by the Caledonian Canal and on the other side by the River Lochy. Bear in mind that facilities decrease as the route unravels, and at the end of the day, Gairlochy only offers a canal-side tearoom and very few accommodation options. During school terms you can catch a bus to Spean Bridge or even back to Fort William, but be sure to check the timetable carefully, or alternatively, ask in advance if your accommodation provider can collect you.

Walkers starting at either the railway station or bus station in **Fort William** have immediate access to the town centre and all its facilities by way of an underpass. To find the start of the Great Glen Way, however, avoid the underpass and walk across Morrison's supermarket car park, then keep left of McDonald's restaurant. The **Old Fort** is located on the far side of a busy roundabout, where a few low walls stand above the shore of **Loch Linnhe**.

S–N route cont. p.39

A **stone monument** marks the start of the Great Glen Way, and the route is marked throughout with signs bearing a 'thistle' logo. Note the design of the monument – two rock types joined at an angle, to mimic the Great Glen Fault.

THE OLD FORT

The first fort on this site was a timber structure, built by General Monck to house 250 men. He referred to it as 'the fort of Inverlochy' in 1654, when writing to advise Oliver Cromwell of its completion. A stone fort was constructed in 1690 by General Mackay, housing 1000 men and defended by fifteen guns. It was named in honour of King William, a member of the Dutch House of Orange, who fought a decisive battle against King James in that year. William ruled Britain jointly with his wife, Mary, James's daughter. General Gordon attacked the fort during the 1715 rebellion, then in 1746 Sir Ewen Cameron attacked it. The fort was largely dismantled and the land bought by the West Highland Railway Company in 1889. They pushed a railway through the site, leaving only the small portion of the original walls seen today, which includes a sally port. The original stone-arched gateway to the fort was rebuilt and now serves as the entrance to a small graveyard off the busy Belford Road in Fort William.

Leave the **Old Fort** and double back round the busy roundabout to find a tarmac pathway on the left side of **McDonald's** restaurant. This is signposted with the 'thistle' logo and soon passes a 'shinty' pitch. (Shinty is a popular Gaelic sport that resembles hockey.) Briefly follow a brick-paved road past a few houses and cross a bridge over the **River Nevis.** Ben Nevis rises far inland to the right, while the waters of Loch Linnhe are a short distance downstream.

Turn left as signposted for the Great Glen Way and follow a gravel path that swings right, running roughly parallel to the tidal **River Lochy.** Alder trees tend to screen the river from sight, and also screen the **Inverlochy** suburbs of Fort William. The path crosses a couple of small **footbridges,** then emerges from the wood into a rushy meadow. Go through a kissing gate and follow the riverside path past a **sports pitch,** then drift right to avoid using a narrow footbridge over the **tailrace** from the Alcan aluminium works. The powerful water flow in the tailrace hits the little footbridge so hard that the water rises up and the structure vibrates! Cross another **bridge** further upstream, then consider a detour beneath the railway line to visit **Inverlochy Castle.**

INVERLOCHY CASTLE

The Comyns were a powerful Scottish family with two branches, the Red Comyns and the Black Comyns. The Red Comyns built Inverlochy Castle (*Gaelic* – Inbhir Lòchaidh) in 1280 and surrounded it with a moat connected to the River Lochy. The four-square thick stone walls are protected by drum towers at each corner, and the largest tower is Comyn's Tower. There was probably a timber-built Great Hall inside the walls. The castle is always open and there is no entrance charge.

A plan of Inverlochy Castle, displayed beside the ruins, shows how it was originally surrounded by a moat.

The Red Comyns and Black Comyns supported John Balliol's claim to the Scottish throne, and therefore attracted the enmity of Robert the Bruce. The MacDonalds supported Bruce, and in 1297 their vessels engaged Comyn vessels off Inverlochy, resulting in the sinking of two ships. The Comyns were later defeated in battle at Inverurie in May 1308, and Bruce granted Inverlochy Castle to the MacDonalds.

In the 15th century the MacDonalds were often in conflict with the Stuarts, who sat on the Scottish throne. Following a MacDonald raid on Inverness, James I sent a force commanded by the Earl or Mar to Inverlochy in 1431. As the army camped by the river they were picked off by MacDonald bowmen from the strategic hill of Tom na Faire, losing a thousand men. In 1645 there was another battle, this time between the Royalist army of Charles I, led by the Marquis of Montrose, with MacDonald support, and a Covenanting force led by the Marquis of Argyll with Campbell support. Again, the strategic hill of Tom na Faire was put to good use by the Royalists, and despite their smaller force, they suffered only 20 casualties, while their opponents suffered 1500.

Following the construction of a wooden fort at Fort William in 1654, which was in turn replaced by a stone fort in 1690, Inverlochy Castle fell from favour. Military might was further consolidated when General Wade built a road from Fort William to Fort Augustus, passing Inverlochy Castle and completed in 1727. The castle was abandoned and was used by the Invergarry Ironworks from 1729 to 1736 as a store for pig iron.

Cross the **Soldier's Bridge** near Inverlochy Castle. This is a long wooden footbridge, mounted on top of a pipe, running parallel to the railway bridge over the **River Lochy.** Walk up to the **B8006 road** and turn left to follow it down past a primary school and a couple of bed and breakfast places to reach the village of **Caol.** Turn left along **Glenmallie Road,** then turn right along **Erracht Drive,** which is flanked by a broad coastal green.

CAOL

Caol (*Gaelic* – Caol Loch Abar) is a village close to The Narrows, where Loch Linnhe turns a right-angle corner and becomes known as Loch Eil. There are a small number of bed and breakfast establishments, a post office, toilets, a couple of shops and take-aways, as well as regular daily bus services to and from neighbouring Fort William, Corpach and Banavie.

After reaching the end of **Erracht Drive,** continue walking along a gravel path hemmed in between the shore of Loch Linnhe and a **sports pitch.** Cross a **footbridge** and follow the path up onto the stout embankment of the **Caledonian Canal.** At this point, either turn right to follow the Great Glen Way onwards, or turn left to explore the nearby village of **Corpach** first.

CORPACH

Corpach (*Gaelic* – A' Chorpaich) is an interesting little village, well worth a visit, overlooking the western sea terminus of the Caledonian Canal. There is public access to the Corpach Sea Lock and Corpach Basin, where boats may be moored while they wait for a favourable tide. The Narrows nearby are dominated by a huge pulp and paper mill, which chews up trees from the surrounding forests. A popular attraction in the village is 'Treasures of the Earth', which focuses on mines, minerals, gemstones and fossils, for those with an interest in geology. Open throughout the year, except Christmas and January, 09.30 to 19.00 in summer and 10.00 to 17.00 in winter (☎01397-772283). There is an entrance charge.

Corpach has a budget bunkhouse and independent hostel, as well as a few bed and breakfast places and a hotel. There is a post office inside the Co-op store, and an ATM outside. Toilets are available in the Kilmallie Hall, when open, while canal users have access to toilets near the canal office. Another shop and a bar are also available, and there are regular daily bus and train services to and from neighbouring Banavie and Fort William.

Follow the course of the **Caledonian Canal** inland, climbing beside the **Corpach Double Lock.** A broad gravel track is followed, flanked on the left by grassy, flowery waterside banks, with fine trees on the right. Note the **overspill weir,** where excess water from the canal flows down into Loch Linnhe. The canal describes a broad and graceful curve to the left, with tall beech trees alongside, often obscuring views of **Caol.** Simply follow the canal-side track until directed by a marker post down a path on the right, not far from a little pub called **Lochy.** Walk along a road, over a level crossing near **Banavie Station,** and turn left to follow the busy A830 towards **Banavie Swing Bridge.** Cross the road without crossing the bridge, then climb uphill in stages beside the celebrated rise of locks known as **Neptune's Staircase.**

BANAVIE

Banavie (*Gaelic* – Banbhaidh) is a little village with only a few facilities, but take note of them as there is nothing else before Gairlochy. The Moorings Hotel and a couple of guest houses are available, along with a canal-side gift shop that also offers teas. There are regular daily bus and train services to and from Corpach and Fort William, as well as a schooldays-only service ahead to Gairlochy.

NEPTUNE'S STAIRCASE

Neptune's Staircase is an inspired name for the tightly packed series of eight canal locks at Banavie. The

Walkers follow a clear canal-side track from Banavie towards Gairlochy and are passed by a cruiser.

arrangement is difficult to see in its entirety, and the best views are those seen in the aerial shots used for postcards. Canal cruisers can pass from top to bottom in about 90 minutes, including passage through the road and rail swing bridges at the bottom, but the time taken can almost double if craft pass through in the other direction at the same time.

The upper part of Neptune's Staircase is **Banavie Top Jetty.** Follow the broad gravel canal-side track onwards, passing through a **gate** beside tall pines. The canal curves gently right and left and for brief periods there are no signs of habitation. A splendid variety of trees flank both banks. It is quite possible to cross the **Sheangain Aqueduct** without noticing, but try and include a few minutes to have a look at it.

SHEANGAIN AQUEDUCT

Use a narrow path to descend from the embankment, then there is a view of three arched tunnels, two arches carrying water from the Allt Sheangain and another arch covering a stone-paved passage for man and his animals.

TOR CASTLE

Not far from the Sheangain Aqueduct, Tor Castle overlooks the River Lochy. It was built by the MacIntoshes, who vacated it towards the end of the 13th century. Some time later it was occupied by the Camerons, sparking a feud between the two clans that spanned some 350 years, continuing even after the Camerons abandoned the property in 1660 and went to settle in Achnacarry.

Continue enjoying the variety of trees alongside, and look across the water to spot a stream feeding water into the canal. Pass a **cottage** where the track rises gently, then falls gently, passing abundant birch trees on the little hill of **Druim na h-Atha.** The track later crosses an **over-spill weir,** where excess water flows down into the River Lochy. Look across the canal to see a knoll crowned with a few pine trees, which is an old **burial ground.** Further along, the canal crosses the **Loy Aqueduct,** built over the **River Loy.**

LOY AQUEDUCT

To see the Loy Aqueduct properly, you must drop down a track on the right well beforehand, then retrace your steps afterwards. It is a splendid structure, with the River Loy flowing through a large central arch, while smaller arches on either side allow passage for man and beast.

Continuing along the canal-side track, the trees diminish and there are gorse bushes alongside for a while, allowing views across small meadows near the **River Lochy.** The attractive white **Moy Swing Bridge** comes into view.

MOY SWING BRIDGE

The Moy Swing Bridge simply allows the farmer from Moy to drive tractors and trailers down to his river-

37

The attractive Moy Swing Bridge is the only bridge on the Caledonian Canal that has to be operated manually.

side meadows. Canal traffic, meanwhile, relies on a keeper to open and close the bridge on demand. However, the bridge is not mechanised, and only one half can be opened manually at a time; hence the need for a small boat so that the keeper can row across and open the other half.

Just beyond **Moy Swing Bridge,** look across the canal to spot another inflowing stream. Also, look out for another knoll with distinctive pine trees on the far bank, which is another old **burial ground.** Tall beech trees again grace the canal-side. Follow the track across an **overspill weir** and enjoy a fine view of the broad and shingly **River Lochy.** Looking back you can see Ben Nevis rising majestically from the Great Glen. Climb past **Gairlochy Bottom Lock** to reach a swing bridge on the narrow B8004 road at **Gairlochy.**

Walkers with time to spare can cross the road and continue along the canal-side track to take a break at the **Telford Tearoom.** Continuing along the track, a slight climb leads past **Gairlochy Top Loch,** where the canal broadens into a mooring basin. Continue beyond a **gate** and follow a grassy path along an embankment to reach a small white **lighthouse** where there is a fine view along the length of **Loch Lochy.** Steps must be retraced to the road afterwards.

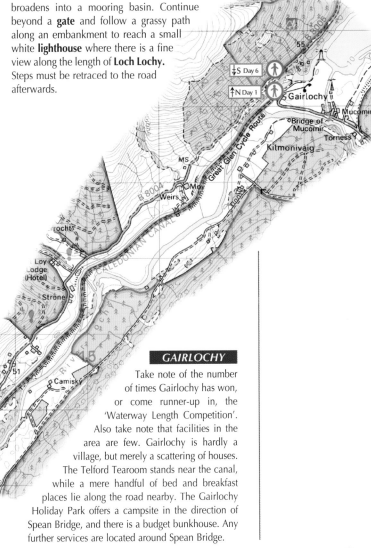

GAIRLOCHY

Take note of the number of times Gairlochy has won, or come runner-up in, the 'Waterway Length Competition'. Also take note that facilities in the area are few. Gairlochy is hardly a village, but merely a scattering of houses. The Telford Tearoom stands near the canal, while a mere handful of bed and breakfast places lie along the road nearby. The Gairlochy Holiday Park offers a campsite in the direction of Spean Bridge, and there is a budget bunkhouse. Any further services are located around Spean Bridge.

A whitewashed pepperpot lighthouse marks where the Caledonian Canal joins Loch Lochy near Gairlochy.

SPEAN BRIDGE

Spean Bridge is 6 kilometres (4 miles) away from Gairlochy. Most of the distance is along and up the quiet B8004 road, passing Mucomir Power Station and the Gairlochy Holiday Park, as well as a couple of bed and breakfast places. The Station House reminds passers-by that a railway once ran through this part of the Great Glen. The road eventually reaches the celebrated Commando Memorial, dating from 1952, on the main A82 road, from where a descent leads to Spean Bridge and its services. A bridge built by General Wade in 1736 was the first to span the rocky gorge beside the village.

There are a few accommodation options around Spean Bridge, including a hotel. There is a post office shop, with an ATM outside, as well as a take-away. There are regular daily Scottish Citylink bus services to and from Fort William, Fort Augustus and Inverness, as well as Rapson's Highland Country buses running to and from Fort William. Bear in mind that there is a schooldays-only bus linking Fort William and Gairlochy with Spean Bridge, but most accommodation providers will provide lifts to and from Gairlochy if given due notice. There are trains to Fort William and Glasgow. The Kingdom of Scotland Visitor Centre at Spean Bridge also serves as the Tourist Information Centre (☎01397-712999).

The Commando Memorial lies off-route, but can be visited by those who head to Spean Bridge for accommodation.

DAY 2

Gairlochy to North Laggan

Start	Gairlochy Bottom Lock – grid ref 176842
Finish	North Laggan – grid ref 300982
Distance	22km (13.5 miles)
Total Ascent	330m (1080ft)
Maps	OS Landranger 34, OS Explorer 400, Harvey Great Glen Way
Terrain	Clear, firm paths, minor roads, forest tracks and a canal-side path.
Refreshments	Telford Tearoom at Gairlochy. The Inn on the Water at Laggan Locks.
Public Transport	There are schooldays-only bus services linking Fort William, Gairlochy and Spean Bridge, which will divert to Achnacarry on request to the driver. Regular daily Scottish Citylink buses link Laggan with Fort William, Fort Augustus and Inverness.

This whole day's walk runs close to the northern shore of Loch Lochy, yet sometimes there are no views across the water. The slopes rising from the loch are often well wooded or forested, so that the water is only glimpsed from time to time. Timber harvesting and replanting in the forests ensure that over time, different places will feature different views. Detours from the Great Glen Way can be considered around Achnacarry, either to see St Ciaran's Church, tucked away in the woods, or to visit the Clan Cameron Museum. This is essentially Cameron country, or at least, it became Cameron country after the Camerons concluded a 350-year feud against the MacIntoshes! The land around Achnacarry was once used as a training ground for commandos. Bear in mind that once you leave Clunes, the only other exit from the long, forested loch-side track is at Laggan. A short stretch along the Caledonian Canal concludes the day's walk, where facilities at the end are very limited.

Leave **Gairlochy Bottom Lock** by crossing the swing bridge, then turn right to follow the **B8005 road,** which

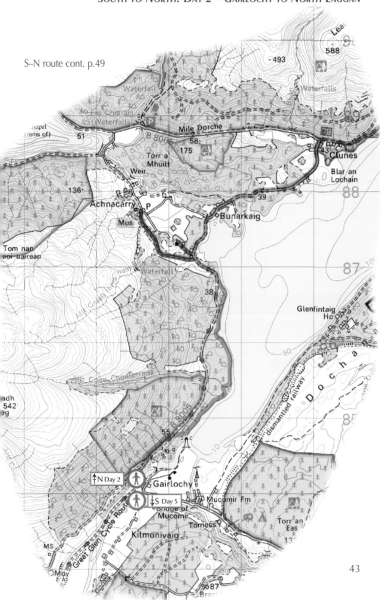

S–N route cont. p.49

43

A view of Loch Lochy near Achnacarry, as a passing shower moves through the glen and leaves a rainbow.

is signposted for Loch Arkaig. Walk up the road and keep straight ahead at a **junction,** then turn left as marked up a **gravel path.** This path undulates across a forested slope just above the road, then later drops down to cross the road. A short, steep descent leads to the shore of **Loch Lochy.** Look back towards Gairlochy to spot a prominent little lighthouse and signs that indicate where the Caledonian Canal joins the loch. Anyone navigating a vessel in darkness would need a clear indication how to leave the loch and enter the canal.

LOCH LOCHY

The level of Loch Lochy was raised 3.65m (12ft) during the construction of the Caledonian Canal. Its surface level is now 28.5m (94ft) above sea level, and its maximum depth is 40.5m (133ft). The loch is just short of 16km (10 miles) in length and only once exceeds 1.5km (1 mile) in width. It is said to be inhabited by a monster known as 'Lizzie', no doubt related to 'Nessie'.

Follow the clear, firm gravel path along the shore, which features fine beech trees. Cross a **footbridge** and note how much moss thrives beneath the trees, covering boulders and fallen tree trunks in soft, bright green, rumpled velvet. Later, birch trees fringe the loch shore and densely packed conifers allow little light to reach the ground. The path drifts away from the shore to cross a footbridge over the **Allt Coire Choille-rais.** Later, the shoreline path crosses **two footbridges** as it runs round a small bay, then climbs gradually across a slope of gnarled oaks, slender birch, beech and alder. Continue along the **B8005 road** to reach a cluster of houses, where a sign invites visitors to make a detour to the **Clan Cameron Museum.**

CLAN CAMERON

The Clan Cameron has a long association with the Great Glen. Originally, there were three families – the McMartins of Letterfinlay, the McGillonies of Strone and the McSorlies of Glen Nevis. The first Chief of the combined families was Donald Dubh, born around 1400, and the most recent is Donald Angus Cameron of Locheil, the 27th Chief. Never shy of battle, the Camerons were described as 'fiercer than fierceness itself'. Their rallying cry was 'Sons of the hounds, come hither and get flesh!' The Camerons moved from Tor Castle to Achnacarry around 1660, and visitors will appreciate the attractions of the location, an easily defended mountain fastness with sheltered pasture.

The 19th Chief, the 'Gentle Locheil', supported Bonnie Prince Charlie in 1745, and in giving support, ensured that many other clans rallied to the cause. Despite early military success, the Prince's forces were soundly beaten at Culloden and Charles was lucky to escape with his life. In retribution for Locheil's support, the Duke of Cumberland destroyed the original timber-built Achnacarry House in 1746, and Locheil fled into exile. The current stone-built Achnacarry House dates from 1802, and the Clan Cameron has distinguished itself by raising generations of soldiery for the Queen's Own Cameron Highlanders. Achnacarry House was occupied by the military for most of the Second World War, when it was the Commando Basic Training Centre, featuring one of the most gruelling military training regimes in the world.

CLAN CAMERON MUSEUM

If you are a Cameron – and that includes members of nearly seventy 'sept' or sub-branch families! – then you should feel obliged to make a detour to the Clan Cameron Museum at Achnacarry. The Museum, housed in a whitewashed 17th-century croft, is open each afternoon from Easter to mid-October, 13.30 to 17.00, but in July and August it is open from 11.00 to 17.00. There should be a notice by the gates on the B8005 road if the museum is open. There is an entrance charge (☎01397-712090, website **www.clan-cameron.org**).

Another short detour could be made to St Ciaran's Church, built in a quiet woodland setting. Watch out for a sign showing the way along a track.

◀ Continue along the **B8005 road,** crossing a bridge over the River Arkaig at **Bunarkaig.** Later, a fine variety

The Clan Cameron Museum is off-route at Achnacarry, but is worth a visit if you can spare the time.

of trees grace the landscape, so that the area is rather like an arboretum. The most striking conifers are the giant redwoods, or sequoias, while the most striking deciduous trees are the copper beeches. The most colourful are undoubtedly the rhododendrons when in bloom, but they do have a habit of choking out other species over time. The land near Loch Lochy is very wet and boggy, supporting profuse growths of bog myrtle. Pass a large white house and modest forestry houses at **Clunes,** then turn right along a **forest track**. This passes a couple of houses and a couple of wooden cabins, one of which is the **Clunes Forest School.** ▶

Go through a tall gate to leave a **car park** and follow the forest track parallel to the shore of **Loch Lochy.** The track undulates and passes commercial conifers, as well as self-seeded alder and birch scrub, along with bracken, brambles and tufts of heather. Pass a small waterfall and a gateway on the **Allt na Molaich** to walk through a more mature part of the forest. The track dips downhill, then climbs gently, passing another **gateway** before descending again. On the next gentle ascent and descent, clear-felling allows good views across Loch Lochy, then after crossing a bridge over the **Allt Glas-Dhoire Mór,** the track passes through another area of mature forest. There is a stretch at a lower level through younger forest, with a margin of alder scrub, where there are more views across the loch.

Pass a tall **gateway** and walk among tall trees, again with no views. Cross a bridge over the **Allt Glas-Dhoire** and drop steeply downhill a short way. The track continues close to the shore of the loch and the trees are remarkably mixed, with conifers, alder and birch. When the track climbs markedly uphill, it is almost exclusively flanked by birch. A junction of tracks is reached near a **communication mast,** where a right turn is made. Go through a **tall gate** and continue straight ahead, passing the access for the **Highland Lodges.** Enjoy views over the head of Loch Lochy on the way downhill, then cross a bridge at **Kilfinnan Farm** to continue along a narrow **tarmac road.**

Occasionally, the Great Glen Way Rangers station themselves at the Forest School and welcome the opportunity to have a chat with walkers.

When the road enters a forest, turn right along another narrow road to pass some wooden lodges, and keep right along the flat to walk along a causeway road, crossing boggy ground beside **Ceann Loch,** to reach **Laggan Locks.** These are double locks, and the Caledonian Canal needs to be crossed at the lock gates. Once across, turn left and walk round a canal-side cottage as directed.

LAGGAN

Laggan (*Gaelic* – Lagan) is a sprawling settlement with no clear centre. South Laggan is the area near Laggan Locks, while North Laggan is closer to the Laggan Swing Bridge, over 2 kilometres (1.25 miles) away. Facilities are limited to the Loch Lochy Youth Hostel, a couple of bed and breakfast places, the 'Eagle', a Dutch barge converted into a pub-restaurant-in-a-boat but known as 'The Inn on the Water', and a bar restaurant at the Great Glen Water Park. Regular daily Scottish Citylink buses link Laggan with Fort William, Fort Augustus and Inverness.

BATTLE OF THE SHIRTS

The seeds of this conflict were sown, as was often the case among Highland clans, with a perceived insult. Ranald Galda, of Clanranald, had been reared among the Frasers, and when he returned to his home a feast was prepared by way of welcome. As seven oxen were slaughtered, Ranald remarked that a few hens would have been sufficient, thus spurning the hospitality of his hosts. They called him 'Ranald of the Hens' and said that he could return to the Frasers if he didn't like it.

It was an uncomfortably hot day in 1544 when 300 Frasers faced a combined force of 600 MacDonalds and Camerons to settle the

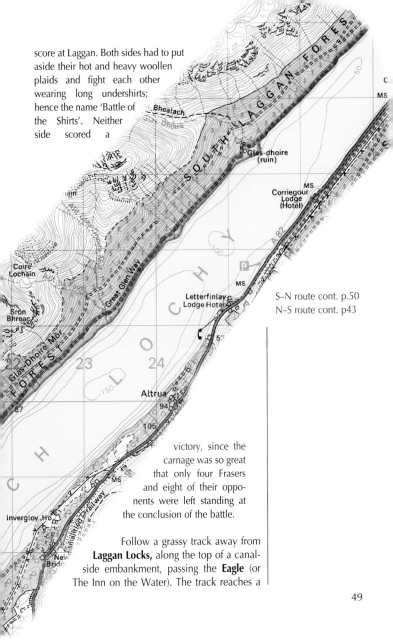

score at Laggan. Both sides had to put aside their hot and heavy woollen plaids and fight each other wearing long undershirts; hence the name 'Battle of the Shirts'. Neither side scored a

S–N route cont. p.50
N–S route cont. p43

victory, since the carnage was so great that only four Frasers and eight of their opponents were left standing at the conclusion of the battle.

Follow a grassy track away from **Laggan Locks,** along the top of a canal-side embankment, passing the **Eagle** (or The Inn on the Water). The track reaches a

49

N–S route cont. p.49

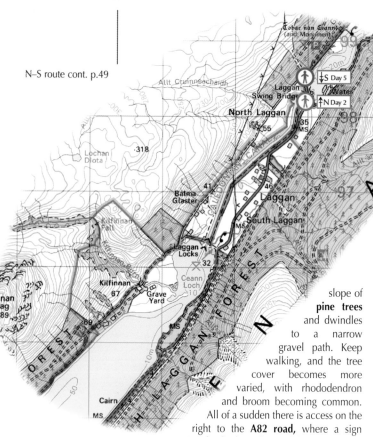

slope of **pine trees** and dwindles to a narrow gravel path. Keep walking, and the tree cover becomes more varied, with rhododendron and broom becoming common. All of a sudden there is access on the right to the **A82 road,** where a sign points back along the road for **Loch Lochy Youth Hostel.** Take care if following the road as it can be very busy.

Continue along the path by crossing a footbridge over a canal feeder, the **Allt an Lagain.** There is later a good view along the canal, from high above a **mooring stage,** where broom, gorse and brambles grow. Follow the path through an area of bracken, to reach the busy **A82 road.** If leaving the route to search for accommodation, take special care while following this road. A sign points left, off-route along the main road, across the Laggan Swing Bridge, for the Well of the Seven Heads Store, if food, drink or an ATM are required. ▶

Some walkers may need to detour to Invergarry in search of accommodation. The quickest and safest way to do this is to catch a bus.

WELL OF THE SEVEN HEADS

Some say it was a deliberate act, while others say it was an accident, but all agree that on 25th September 1663, Alexander MacDonald, Chief of Keppoch, and his brother Ranald, were killed by seven others during a clan dispute. While most of their kinsfolk seemed content to let the matter rest, Iain Lom, the Keppoch Bard, called for revenge, enlisting the support of MacDonald of Glengarry and Sir James MacDonald of Sleat. After two years, the seven culprits were tracked down to Inverlair, where they were slain and beheaded. The severed heads were washed in a well beside Loch Oich, then displayed at Invergarry Castle before being taken to Gallows Hill in Edinburgh on 7th December 1665. The Well of the Seven Heads is now enclosed in stone and bears a monument. The monument is crowned with seven unhappy-looking heads, surmounted by a hand holding a dagger. The tale of murder and revenge is carved around all four sides in English, Gaelic, French and Latin.

INVERGARRY

The village of Invergarry is on the 'wrong' side of Loch Oich to the Great Glen Way, but some walkers may need to go there if they cannot secure lodgings around Laggan. A small range of lodgings ranges from hostel to hotel accommodation. Regular daily Scottish Citylink buses link Invergarry with Fort William and Inverness. The Glengarry Visitor Centre, open from Easter to September, 10.30 to 16.30, has a small entrance charge and also operates as a Tourist Information Centre (☎01809-501424).

The 'Eagle' is also known as 'The Inn on the Water',
offering a floating bar and restaurant at South Laggan (Day 2).

DAY 3

North Laggan to Fort Augustus

Start	North Laggan – grid ref 300982
Finish	Fort Augustus Swing Bridge – grid ref 379092
Distance	14km (9 miles)
Total Ascent	30m (100ft)
Maps	OS Landranger 34, OS Explorer 400, Harvey Great Glen Way
Terrain	Tracks and paths beside Loch Oich can be wet and muddy. A clear and firm canal-side track leads onwards to Fort Augustus.
Refreshments	A restaurant and bar is located at the Great Glen Water Park. A couple of tearooms lie off-route at Aberchalder. There are plenty of restaurants, cafés, take-aways and bars around Fort Augustus.
Public Transport	Regular daily Scottish Citylink buses link Laggan and Fort Augustus with Fort William and Inverness. The Loch Ness Express ferry links Fort Augustus with Dochgarroch, near Inverness.

This is a splendid day's walk, where the walls of the Great Glen rise closer to hand and there are often views of high mountains further beyond. The Great Glen Way leaves North Laggan and continues along the southern shore of Loch Oich, where the richly wooded slopes are protected as a nature reserve. The course of an old railway line, as well as a stretch of General Wade's military road, are followed along the shore. At Aberchalder, there is an opportunity to admire the cunningly designed Bridge of Oich. Another lovely stretch of the Caledonian Canal leads onwards, gradually locking down until a steep flight of five locks drops down through Fort Augustus into Loch Ness. The bustling village of Fort Augustus has several points of interest and it is well worth discovering some of them during the evening. As this is a short day's walk, some walkers choose to pass straight through Fort Augustus and continue along the Great Glen Way to Invermoriston.

A quiet road leads from the busy **A82 road** near the **Laggan Swing Bridge** to the **Great Glen Water Park,** on the shores of **Loch Oich,** where there is a bar and restaurant surrounded by wooden holiday chalets. There is no need to follow the access road as directed to reach the bar and restaurant; simply stay on the road marked as the Great Glen Way and the building is quite close to hand just as the route leaves the road.

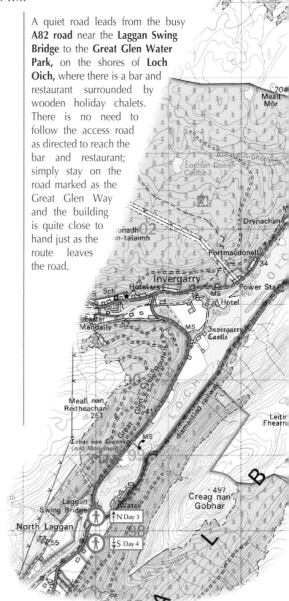

S–N route cont. p.61

Head right up a track into **woods** where there are clumps of rhododendron. The track becomes aligned to an old **railway trackbed,** which features some cuttings where the ground can be wet and muddy. The surroundings are vividly green and are managed as a **nature reserve.** Step down from the old railway trackbed later and go through a **gate** to follow the course of an old **military road** along the shore of **Loch Oich.** Keep dogs under control as sheep graze around here.

LEITERFEARN FOREST NATURE RESERVE

Leiterfearn features a lush, damp, vibrantly green woodland that is a mixture of ash, birch, elm and hazel. The steep slopes support cushions of moss and delicate ferns, as well as flowers in spring and fungi in autumn. It has the appearance of a jungle, yet it has been cut back twice to accommodate a road and railway. General Wade pushed a road through the woods around 1725, while the Invergarry and Fort Augustus Railway Company pushed a railway through, which opened in 1903. Both routes fell from favour, the road switching to the other side of the loch and the railway being abandoned in 1946.

A fishing trawler passes from Loch Oich towards
Laggan Swing Bridge on its way through the Caledonian Canal.

LOCH OICH

This is the smallest of the three lochs linked by the Caledonian Canal (not counting the much smaller Kytra Loch). It measures 6.5km (4 miles) in length and is only 0.5km (0.3 miles) across at its widest point. Loch Oich's greatest depth is 40.5m (133ft), but it had to be deepened at both ends to accommodate traffic using the Caledonian Canal. The surface level of the loch is 32m (105ft), which is also the summit level for the canal.

There are views across the loch from time to time when the trees thin out, and the ruins of **Invergarry Castle** might be seen on the far shore. Watch out for a crenelated **concrete arch** on the right, which supports the old railway trackbed. Pass the old whitewashed **Leiterfearn Cottage** and follow a grassy track through a small meadow. The track runs through woods and briefly touches the shore again, before rising steeply to avoid a **cliff.** Climb through a rocky, mossy cutting, crossing over an old railway tunnel. When the track runs gently downhill, watch out for a miniature **iron aqueduct** on the left, carrying water across the old line. Cross a **bridge** at a small waterfall and reach a couple of **gates.**

Ahead lies the **Aberchalder Estate Road,** which may be of interest to those who wish to reach a couple of bed and breakfast places, and a couple of cafés. These are listed on a sign and are all within easy reach of **Aberchalder Lodge.** The Great Glen Way, however, turns left at the gates, then crosses an old railway bridge over the **Calder Burn.** Turn left at a kissing gate to follow a path beside **Loch Oich,** then cross a ladder stile and continue along a canal-side path to reach the **Aberchalder Swing Bridge.** Cross over the busy **A82 road** with care.

BRIDGE OF OICH

It is worth leaving the Great Glen Way for a few minutes and crossing the Aberchalder Swing Bridge

The Bridge of Oich is a curious structure, patented as a 'double cantilever' and built on the 'taper principle'.

to reach the Bridge of Oich. An older bridge was swept away in devastating floods during 1849, when the embankment of the Caledonian Canal was also breached. Five years elapsed before a new bridge was built, by a brewer-turned-engineer called James Dredge, from Bath. The Bridge of Oich looks like a

slender suspension bridge, but was actually patented as a 'double cantilever', built on the 'taper principle'. The supporting chains gradually diminish as they spread outwards from the stout granite pillars that support them, and hold very little weight in the middle of the bridge. Apparently, if the bridge was ever severed in the middle, it would remain standing. The Bridge of Oich carried traffic up to 1932, but the busy A82 road now crosses a more solid-looking stone bridge nearby.

After crossing the A82 road, pass a **cottage** and follow a clear track beside the **Caledonian Canal.** Look across the water to spot a large **overspill weir** feeding excess water into the River Oich. When **Cullochy Lock** is reached, cross over the lock gates to pick up and follow a **track** on the other side of the canal. A variety of trees flank the canal, but there are several particularly tall and graceful birch trees. The canal broadens considerably where **Kytra Loch** was incorporated into its course. An **overspill weir** has to be crossed later, and this could mean wet feet if there is excess water in the canal, though this would be a very rare occurrence.

Pass **Kytra Lock,** where tall pine trees flank the canal on both sides. The pines soon give way to more mixed

An attractive lock-keeper's cottage at Cullochy Lock near Aberchalder. The canal has to be crossed at this point.

The Caledonian Canal is considerably broader where the little Kytra Loch has been incorporated into its course.

woodland cover, and there are glimpses of the **River Oich** from time to time, as both the canal and the river pursue parallel courses. Hazel trees are abundant beside the track, while later a fine row of pine trees grows along the opposite bank, after the canal bends gradually to the left and passes a **power line.** A covered overspill weir allows more excess water to fall into the River Oich, then the canal bends to the right and the buildings of **Fort Augustus** can be seen ahead. The village sits on either side of a fine flight of five locks stepping down towards Loch Ness.

FORT AUGUSTUS

The earliest settlement at Fort Augustus (*Gaelic* – Cill Chuimein) was founded in the 6th century by monks from Iona, led by St Cumin. Precious little else is recorded about the place until, in the aftermath of the Jacobite Rising of 1715, a fort was constructed on the site now occupied by the Lovat Hotel. When General

Wade built a military road through the area in 1726, the fort was moved to where the Abbey now stands. Fort Augustus was named after William Augustus, Duke of Cumberland, and was destroyed at the beginning of the Jacobite Rising of 1745. 'Butcher' Cumberland had it rebuilt while engaged in a brutal campaign to suppress the Highland clans. The site was given to the Benedictines in 1876, who built the Abbey, vacating it in 1997. The Abbey has since been redeveloped and there is no longer any public access to it.

N–S route cont. p.55

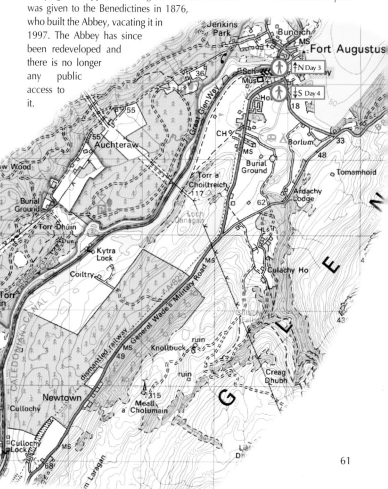

The bustling tourist village of Fort Augustus is halfway along the Great Glen Way. It offers plenty of accommodation, from a campsite and humble bed and breakfast places to fine hotels. There is a bank, but if an ATM is needed, then go to the Spar shop. There is a post office and a choice of food and gift shops. There are several bars, restaurants, cafés and take-aways. Toilets are located beside the Tourist Information Centre (☎01320-366367). There are regular daily bus services to Fort William and Inverness. Cruises on Loch Ness are also available, as well as the Loch Ness Express ferry to Inverness. An interesting rural attraction lying close to the village is the Highland and Rare Breeds Croft, sign-posted from the bridge, open 10.00 to 18.00 except Saturday, March to October. There is an entrance charge (☎01320-366433).

CALEDONIAN CANAL VISITOR CENTRE

As walkers descend the flight of five locks through Fort Augustus, metal disks along the way pose all sorts of questions about the Caledonian Canal, its history, construction and use. Visitors who want to find the answers are directed to the Caledonian Canal Visitor Centre, just across the road. A small exhibition space can be explored, there are books on sale about the canal, while British Waterways Scotland staff are on hand to deal with any queries. The centre is open 09.30 to 17.30, April to October, and entry is free (☎01320-366493).

GREAT GLEN WAY RANGERS

The Great Glen Way Rangers, who maintain the route you are following, have an office in the forest at Auchterawe, not far from Fort Augustus. They welcome feedback from walkers and are keen to hear about problems experienced along the route so that they can address them. Contact: Great Glen Way Rangers, Auchterawe, Fort Augustus, PH32 4BT; ☎01320-366633.

DAY 4

Fort Augustus to Invermoriston

Start	Fort Augustus Swing Bridge – grid ref 379092
Finish	Glenmoriston Arms Hotel, Invermoriston – grid ref 420168
Distance	13km (8 miles)
Total Ascent	300m (985ft)
Maps	OS Landranger 34, OS Explorer 416S, Harvey Great Glen Way
Terrain	Forest tracks and paths with some short, steep slopes.
Refreshments	There are plenty of bars, restaurants, cafés and take-aways around Fort Augustus. Invermoriston has a hotel with a bar-restaurant and one other restaurant.
Public Transport	Regular daily Scottish Citylink buses link Fort Augustus and Invermoriston with Inverness and Fort William. The Loch Ness Express ferry links Fort Augustus with Dochgarroch, near Inverness.

This is a very short day's walk; indeed, it could easily be covered in a morning or an afternoon, and some walkers simply add it to the previous day's walk if they are trying to complete the Great Glen Way in a hurry. This short day's walk could allow walkers a whole morning to explore Fort Augustus, maybe including a cruise on Loch Ness in order to gain a greater appreciation of its vastness. While the Great Glen Way often runs close to Loch Ness, forested slopes often shield it from view, so walkers see less of it than they might imagine. Invermoriston is a tiny village and it is quickly explored in the evening. If planning to stay there, it is wise to book lodgings in advance, although it is a simple matter to catch a bus elsewhere in search of accommodation.

Leave **Fort Augustus** along the busy **A82 road** in the direction of Inverness, crossing a bridge over the River Oich and passing the Tourist Information Centre. Turn left up a minor road called **Bunoich Brae,** or rather, up a tarmac path making a short cut just beforehand. Follow

63

A left turn at the junction, for Jenkins Park and Auchterawe, leads to the Great Glen Way Rangers' base.

S–N route cont. p.67

the road uphill, keeping straight ahead at a **junction.** ◀

The narrow road passes a couple of bed and breakfast places and runs down towards the busy main road.

Just before the main road, at **Three Bridges,** turn left along a **riverside path.** Cross a **foot-bridge** in a

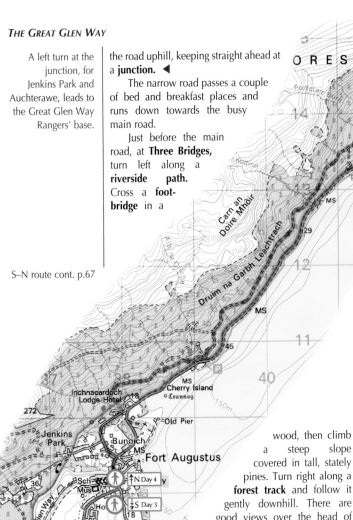

wood, then climb a steep slope covered in tall, stately pines. Turn right along a **forest track** and follow it gently downhill. There are good views over the head of Loch Ness near Fort Augustus. Plenty of birch trees grow among the conifers, and the track leads downhill through a **gate,** almost back onto the main road again at **Allt na Criche.**

64

Turn left to follow another track away from the main road, quickly swinging right to cross a tumbling **stream.** The woods are mixed, with some fine oaks and birch, but as the broad track bends and climbs, avoiding a left turn, there are more conifers. Pass a **gate** and climb among tall conifers, with lush margins of heather, bilberry, mosses, ferns and wood sorrel. There is a slight dip in the track, then keep straight ahead at a **junction** to climb gradually among tall trees. Walk downhill, then uphill, then enjoy good views over a slope of young trees, across Loch Ness to the rugged hill of Beinn a' Bhacaidh. Another gentle rise leads to a **stone-slab seat,** where views both ways along Loch Ness seem endless.

LOCH NESS

Walkers will seldom be able to see the whole of Loch Ness, but will often catch a glimpse of some part of it. The deep trough it occupies has been filled with water ever since the end of the last Ice Age around 10,000 years ago, and it reflects enough light to brighten even the dullest days in the Great Glen. Six major rivers carry water into Loch Ness, from a part of the Highlands known for high rainfall, explaining why the River Ness flows so powerfully past Inverness. Here are some facts and figures to help appreciate its full extent:

- Catchment area – 1800 square kilometres (700 square miles)
- Surface area – 56 square kilometres (22 square miles)
- Length – 37 kilometres (23 miles)
- Width – 3 kilometres (1.9 miles)
- Shoreline length – 86 kilometres (53.5 miles)
- Volume – 7.5 cubic kilometres (1.8 cubic miles)
- Maximum depth – 230m (755ft)
- Surface level – 16m (52ft) above sea level

The River Oich is flanked by woodlands as it flows from Fort Augustus towards the broad waters of Loch Ness.

There is only one island in Loch Ness, the diminutive Cherry Island near Fort Augustus, which is actually an ancient man-made island dwelling, or crannog. More astonishing facts include oft-repeated statements that the volume of water in the loch exceeds that of all the lakes and reservoirs in England and Wales, and is sufficient to immerse the entire population of the world!

Campers should walk down the main track in order to reach the Loch Ness Caravan and Camping Park at Rubha Bàn, with the minimum amount of walking along the A82.

Views are lost on a descent into tall forest, where a concrete bridge spans a waterfall on the **Allt a' Mhuilinn.** There is a gentle ascent with a view across a younger part of the forest, again taking in the hill of Beinn a' Bhacaidh across Loch Ness. Walk gently downhill and lose the views in the forest. Cross a concrete bridge over **Portclair Burn,** then cross a dip in the track. Climb gently to cross another concrete bridge over a small **waterfall.** There is a good view of Loch Ness on the way downhill, overlooking a clear-felled slope, then views are lost and the gentle descent becomes steeper. The main track suddenly swings sharp right, so keep straight ahead up another track. ◄

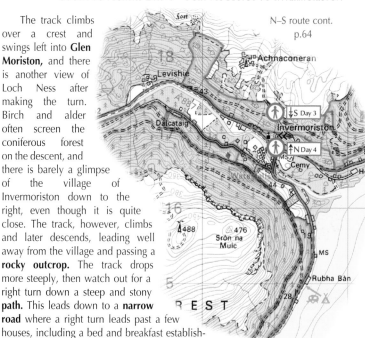

N–S route cont. p.64

The track climbs over a crest and swings left into **Glen Moriston,** and there is another view of Loch Ness after making the turn. Birch and alder often screen the coniferous forest on the descent, and there is barely a glimpse of the village of Invermoriston down to the right, even though it is quite close. The track, however, climbs and later descends, leading well away from the village and passing a **rocky outcrop.** The track drops more steeply, then watch out for a right turn down a steep and stony **path.** This leads down to a **narrow road** where a right turn leads past a few houses, including a bed and breakfast establishment, at **Dalcataig.**

The Falls of Moriston can be admired from the Old Bridge, also known as Telford's Bridge, near Invermoriston.

67

The road is mostly wooded, rising and falling gently, passing the wooden **Dalcataig Chalets.** Follow the road down to a junction with the main **A82 road** and turn left, but note the ravaged remains of **Telford's Bridge** spanning the River Moriston, and the splendid Moriston Falls that spill beneath it. The main road runs into the little village of **Invermoriston.**

TELFORD'S BRIDGE

The ramshackle remains of Telford's Bridge, also known as the Old Bridge, could be crossed in preference to the main road bridge, but take care as the masonry is in a bad state of repair. Despite being nothing more than a standard double-span stone arch, its construction spanned several years from 1805 until 1813, owing to a 'languid and inattentive contractor' and 'idle workers'. The bridge is one of more than a thousand associated with Telford.

The Glenmoriston Arms Hotel was a drover's inn, dating from 1740, and offers accommodation, food and drink.

INVERMORISTON

Invermoriston (*Gaelic* – Inbhir Mor Eason) has only a few facilities, but at the end of the day these prove most welcome. The Glenmoriston Arms Hotel is very

prominent. It was originally a drovers' inn, dating from 1740, and the oldest parts are around the bar and reception area. Johnson and Boswell stayed there while planning a trip to the Hebrides in 1773. There are a few bed and breakfast places in and around the village, as well as the Glenmoriston Stores Post Office, Pig's Nose Coffee Shop and Restaurant, and the Clog and Craft Shop. Toilets are available inside the Glenmoriston Millennium Hall, when open. Regular daily Scottish Citylink buses link Invermoriston with Inverness and Fort William, as well as the Isle of Skye.

THE SEVEN MEN OF GLEN MORISTON

The date was July 27th 1746, when Bonnie Prince Charlie was on the run after the crushing defeat at the Battle of Culloden. Pursued by 'Butcher' Cumberland, and with a bounty of £30,000 on his head, Charles had not eaten for two days and was clad in rags by the time he reached Glen Moriston. Coming upon a crude hut and ravenously hungry, he was warned by his companions not to seek food or shelter in case he was recognised. Charles declared 'I had better be killed like a man than starved like a fool', and made his way to the hut. The seven men inside were mere outlaws, and one of them recognised him, but to their credit, they spurned the chance to claim the bounty and risked their lives to feed and shelter him. Meanwhile, on the road through Glen Moriston, an Edinburgh merchant named Roderick MacKenzie, who bore a passing resemblance to the Bonnie Prince, was shot at by troops. As he died he declared, 'Alas, you have killed your prince', and this ruse was sufficient to buy enough time for Charles to be smuggled out of the country.

DAY 5

Invermoriston to Drumnadrochit

Start	Glenmoriston Arms Hotel, Invermoriston – grid ref 420168
Finish	Tourist Information Centre, Drumnadrochit – grid ref 507299
Distance	23km (14 miles)
Total Ascent	600m (1970ft)
Maps	OS Landrangers 26 & 34, OS Explorer 416S, Harvey Great Glen Way
Terrain	Forest tracks and paths. Moorland road.
Refreshments	Hotel-restaurant and coffee shop at Invermoriston. Plenty of restaurants, cafés and take-aways in Drumnadrochit.
Public Transport	Regular daily Scottish Citylink buses link Invermoriston and Drumnadrochit with Inverness and Fort William, and these services can also be accessed at Loch Ness Youth Hostel at Alltsigh.

The whole of this day's walk is alongside Loch Ness, but densely forested slopes ensure that there are only occasional views of it along the way. There is also more climbing than in previous days, though any steep slopes quickly level out, and most of the day is spent on clear and obvious forest tracks. A viewpoint can be accessed early in the day by making a short diversion, and it offers a glimpse of what the landscape looked like before commercial forests were planted. There are extensive views along Loch Ness later, though these pass completely from view as the route climbs higher and shifts well away from the water. Drumnadrochit is reached at the end of the day, where the principal attractions are two rival exhibitions devoted to Loch Ness and its 'monster'. Be sure to arrive in good time if intending to visit either or both of these places, as they are both packed with plenty of interest.

Leave **Invermoriston** via the **A887 road,** signposted for Kyle of Lochalsh, referred to locally as the Skye Road.

Turn right at the **Clog & Craft Shop,** where a milestone warns 'Last Clog Shop before Skye – 52 miles'. A steep and narrow **zigzag road** climbs up a well-wooded slope bearing sycamore, beech, oak and birch, with a holly understorey at a higher level. Densely planted conifers flank the road before it crosses a **bridge** over a stream. Turn right almost immediately to follow a **forest track** across another bridge over the same stream.

The track makes a gentle ascent among closely packed trees, then while crossing a crest, a thinner part of the plantation reveals some of the former heather cover and low rocky outcrops.

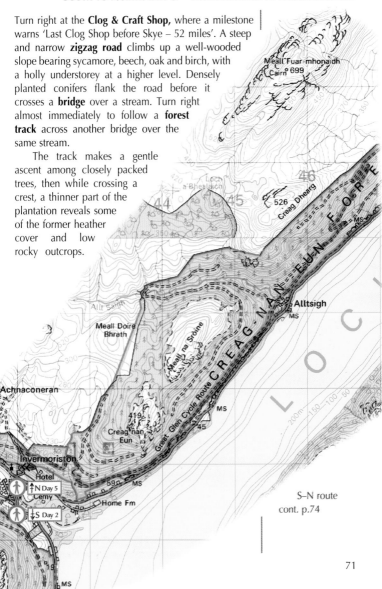

S–N route
cont. p.74

71

The track swings left, then right, to cross a concrete bridge over the **Allt Coinneag.** Follow the track through a tall **gateway,** then turn right downhill from a junction. Turn right at another junction as marked, but also consider turning left as signposted for a nearby **viewpoint.** This short detour reveals a narrow path winding up a slope covered in ling and bell heather to reach the crude **Stone Seat,** where there is a fine view over Loch Ness. The village of Invermoriston, despite being close at hand, is completely hidden from view. Retrace your steps to the junction.

Walk down a narrow and bendy **forest path** as marked, landing on a **forest track** below. Turn left and follow the track gently downhill, with only occasional glimpses of Loch Ness. A post draws attention to the **Stone Cave,** said to have been built to offer shelter to a washerwoman on her frequent journeys between Alltsigh and Invermoriston. It still offers splendid shelter. Later, there is a slight climb to a bend where there is a good **viewpoint** revealing the length of Loch Ness, but also turn around and admire the fine variety of trees stacked against the cliffs of **Creag nan Eun.**

Continue down the track, passing a rugged slope of gorse bushes where no forest trees were ever planted, losing views of the loch. Keep straight ahead at a **junction of tracks** beside a rock cutting, climbing gently for a while. Walk gently downhill, uphill, then downhill along a track fringed with broom. Drop more steeply from a **junction of tracks** and cross a concrete bridge over a rocky gorge at **Alltsigh.** There is a waterfall in the gorge, as well as a variety of trees, while a diligent search reveals an old packhorse bridge.

ALLTSIGH

A sign simply states SYHA and points down a track and through a gate. The track passes a white house and quickly reaches the busy A82 road beside Loch Ness. Immediately to the left is Briarbank bed and breakfast, while further away to the right is Loch Ness

Youth Hostel and a bus stop. The hostel occupies a site offering splendid views across the loch.

Those who don't need to detour to **Alltsigh** can simply walk straight up a **forest track** as marked, climbing among tall conifers with no views. Later, there are good views back through the Great Glen. The track bends sharp left and sharp right as it climbs above **Primrose Bay,** with views through the glen becoming even more extensive, as well as taking in the village of Foyers across the loch.

The track bends quickly left and right to climb further, then there is another sharp left and sharp right turn, where views through the Great Glen stretch far beyond Fort Augustus to reveal a glimpse of distant Loch Oich. Looking far across Loch Ness, the remote Monadh Liath range rolls southwards into the distance. Nearby clear-felled slopes are profusely covered in rosebay willowherb.

The track undulates close to 300m (985ft) above **Ruskich Wood** and views are lost as the trees grow taller. Cross a concrete bridge over the **Allt Ghiubhnais** and descend gently. There is often a grassy strip along the

A view of Loch Ness and Beinn a' Bhacaidh from a point near Alltsigh and the Loch Ness Youth Hostel.

73

N–S route
cont. p.71

S–N route cont.
p.76

middle of the track, which ends abruptly at a turning space. Continue along a **narrow path,** which is rough and stony in places, and may be muddy in some parts when wet. There are views directly across Loch Ness to Foyers, looking over the tops of young forest trees. There are also tall birch trees and slopes of bracken, broom and heather. Views are lost as the trees alongside grow taller, and eventually a turning space is reached on another **forest track.**

Looking back from Ancarraig towards Balbeg and the humped hill of Meall Fuar-mhonaidh.

Continue straight along the track, climbing slightly before heading quite steeply downhill. Again, the track often has a grassy strip along its middle. Watch out for an opening in the trees on the right, where there is a view north-east along Loch Ness. Also watch out for markers revealing a clear **path** rising to the left. This is a little rugged in places and may be muddy when wet. It is

N–S route cont.
p.74

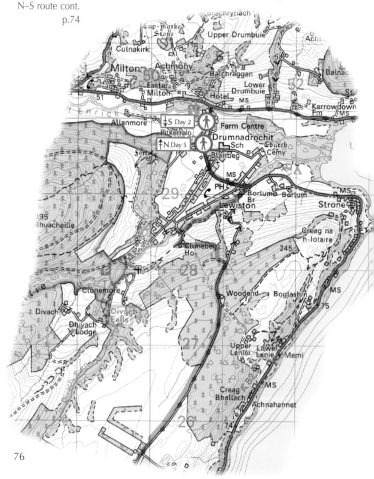

fringed with young birch trees and leads through a **gate** in a deer fence. Swing left uphill among tall oaks to reach a gate on a **grassy gap** below the wooded knoll bearing the remains of an ancient fort called **Dùn Scriben.** There is a view of a tiny portion of Loch Ness. Follow the track a short distance downhill to cross the **Grotaig Burn,** then head up through a gate and follow the track upstream to reach another gate and a **narrow road.** To the left is a pottery, at the end of the road, while to the right is a **car park.**

Turn right to walk through the car park, then follow a path running parallel to a minor road around **Balbeg.** There are occasional glimpses of Loch Ness while passing isolated houses and farms. Look back to see the humped hills of Meall Fuar-mhonaidh and Creag Dhearg. Follow the road past the **Ancarraig Lodges,** then gorse grows on either side as the road rises up a boggy moorland slope. Later, a swathe of rough grassland lies to the right, while improved pasture lies to the left. The road undulates over 250m (820ft) on a **heather moorland,** and there is another path running parallel. The road runs into a forest and heads gently downhill, but after passing a house at **Woodend** it falls more steeply.

Turn left as signposted for the Great Glen Way. Go through a gate and walk down a **forest track** to another gate. Turn right down a broad **forest path,** which soon turns left. There is a brief glimpse of Drumnadrochit before the path enters a dense part of the forest, later crossing a footbridge to go through a **gate.** There are further views of the village as the path runs down across a bracken-clad slope dotted with fine oaks. Swing right to reach **Clunebeg Lodge** and follow the access track downhill from **Clunebeg House,** admiring tall beech and oaks alongside. The track levels out beside the bouldery **River Coiltie.** Houses seen on the far side are part of the village of **Lewiston.** A variety of densely packed trees usually screen the river from view as the track runs to join a minor road at a big sign for the Clunebeg Estate. Follow the road straight ahead to reach a picnic area at a junction with the busy **A82 road.** ▶

Walkers who wish to reach the campsite at **Borlum,** or the celebrated ruins of **Urquhart Castle,** should turn right and follow the path running parallel to the main road.

Turn left to follow the **A82 road** across the River
Coiltie to reach **Lewiston.** Signs alert walkers to a few
offers of food, drink and accommodation, then the road
bends gradually right, passing the Drum take-away and
Co-op, where there is an ATM, to reach the nearby village
of **Drumnadrochit,** which has a greater range of services.

DRUMNADROCHIT

Drumnadrochit (*Gaelic* – Druim na Drochaid) is a
busy little village with plenty to catch the attention of
passing tourists. Two attractions vying for attention
are the 'Original' Loch Ness Monster Visitor Centre,
at the Loch Ness Lodge Hotel, open all year
(☎01456-450432), and the 'Official' Loch Ness
2000 Exhibition, at the Drumnadrochit Hotel, open
all year (☎01456-450573). There are entrance
charges to both places. Whatever you want to know
about Loch Ness and its 'monster', this is the place to
take on board all the opinions, then you can make up
your own mind. If nothing more than a 'Nessie'
souvenir is required, a handful of gift shops around
the village deal in the widest selection of products.

There is accommodation to suit every pocket,
from hotels to guest houses and bed and breakfast
places, with an independent hostel in Lewiston and a
campsite further along the road at Borlum. Most facilities are clustered round the village green at
Drumnadrochit. There is a bank with an ATM, a post
office store, toilets, bars, restaurants, cafés and take-
aways. There are souvenir and gift shops, as well as
a Tourist Information Centre (☎01456-459050).
Regular daily Scottish Citylink buses link
Drumnadrochit with Inverness and Fort William.
Cruises on Loch Ness are also available.

URQUHART CASTLE

Urquhart Castle is 2km (1.25 miles) off-route, or
3.25km (2 miles) from Drumnadrochit, perched on

A floral model of Urquhart Castle occupies pride of place on a pleasant green in the middle of Drumnadrochit.

Strone Point overlooking Loch Ness. It can be reached safely on foot as there is a path beside the busy A82 road, and Scottish Citylink buses serve both Drumnadrochit and the castle. The situation is splendid and it is a renowned place for those keeping a lookout for the Loch Ness Monster! Once one of the largest castles in Scotland, Urquhart Castle's sprawling ruins take time to explore. A visitor centre offers a thorough grounding in its construction and history, plus a café. Urquhart Castle is open all year and there is an entrance charge (☎01456-450551).

A Bronze Age promontory fort once stood on Strone Point, and there were other defensive structures on the site before Urquhart Castle was built in the 13th century. Its history is one of intense conflict, in which English and Scots alternately occupied it, with William Wallace and Robert the Bruce each holding the property for a time. Buchan, son of Robert II, held the castle from 1390, ruling with brutal force, and frequently robbing churches. In the 15th and 16th centuries the MacDonalds launched raids on the castle, which was later held by the Grants. The bulk of the damage to the castle was done with explosives in 1692, which prevented it becoming a Jacobite stronghold in subsequent years.

Visitors cross a wooden gangway across a defensive ditch, and pass through a gatehouse. However, in the past, most people approaching the castle would have done so through a watergate from Loch Ness. The centrepiece of Urquhart Castle is a stout and impressive tower house, but be sure to take note of the complex arrangement of the ruined defensive walls that surround the site. The best vantage point is of course from the top of the tower house.

Walkers who can't spare the time to detour to the castle can console themselves by studying an interesting floral model of the castle in the middle of the village green in Drumnadrochit.

DAY 6

Drumnadrochit to Inverness

Start	Tourist Information Centre, Drumnadrochit – grid ref 507299
Finish	Inverness Castle – grid ref 666451
Distance	29km (18 miles)
Total Ascent	500m (1640ft)
Maps	OS Landranger 26, OS Explorer 416N, Harvey Great Glen Way
Terrain	A road walk, followed by forest and moorland tracks. A longer road walk, followed by urban pathways through green spaces to the finish.
Refreshments	Drumnadrochit and Inverness.
Public Transport	Regular daily Scottish Citylink buses link Drumnadrochit with Inverness and Fort William. Approaching Inverness, there are several points where local city bus services can be accessed. Long-distance bus and rail services are available from Inverness, and there is an airport nearby.

This is the longest day's walk on the Great Glen Way, and the highest point is crossed around 380m (1245ft) in the Abriachan Forest. The forest is managed by the local community, who have cleared, marked and signposted a network of trails. The area is proving popular with visitors and school parties. The route is rather distant from the Great Glen and follows the course of an old drove road, which passes through an interesting remnant Scots pine forest. By the time the route descends back into the glen, it is on the outskirts of Inverness. Take care over route-finding through the suburbs, where one green space after another is linked to provide a route into the very heart of the city. Once the finish is reached at Inverness Castle, there is a chance to look back along the route through the Great Glen and reflect on your journey across Scotland.

Leave **Drumnadrochit** by following the main **A82 road** in the direction of Inverness. Stay on the pavement on the left-hand side throughout, passing a handful of bed and

S–N route cont. p.86

Druim Bà

Lochlait

271

Càrn na · 434 Leitire

Loch na Guíce

370

Rivoulich

Achpopuli

391

Creag Ard

Cnoc Snàtaig 418

Meall na △ 465 h-Eilrig

Corr

Loch Glanaidh

Cnoc Fhearchair 410

Hut Circles & Field Systems

Garbeg

Brachryriach

Wester Achtuie

Upper Drumbuie

Achtuie 376

Great Glen Way

52

Creag Nay

Achmony

Balchraggan

Lower Drumbuie

Balnacraig

MS

Easter Milton

Hotel

MS

St Ninians

Tychat

54

5

Kerrowdown Fm

24

MS

↑N Day 6

Farm Centre

↓S Day 1

Drumnadrochit

Sch

Church Cemy

Urquhart Bay

MS

PH

Borluma Br

Borlum

MS

Lewiston

Strone

82

breakfast places. There is access on the other side of the road for **Urquhart Bay Harbour,** for cruises on Loch Ness. Turn left up the access road for **Temple House,** then quickly turn left again, up through a gate, to follow a path beside a tall fence to pass the house. There is a brief glimpse of Urquhart Castle across Urquhart Bay on Loch Ness. The path runs parallel to the road, then climbs through small gates and crosses a narrow access road that leads up to **Tychat.** Continue through woods, climbing through more small gates, then follow a path across a **grassy slope** overlooking a stretch of Loch Ness, again with a view of Urquhart Castle.

A **gate** leads into dense forest, but the path is clear and obvious. There is a brief glimpse of Loch Ness just before a **footbridge,** then the path climbs gradually. Little light reaches the forest floor, so only moss and wood sorrel grow alongside the path. When the path turns sharply left and right, it climbs through a more open area of grass and bracken, with several **birch trees** growing. The path runs more or less level for a while, then climbs, before descending to cross **stepping stones** over a small burn. A short ascent leads onto a **forest track.**

Follow the track onwards, undulating at first, then climbing gradually up a clear-felled slope. There are views over Loch Ness, but they aren't particularly good, and at a higher level the track drifts well away from the loch. Go through a **tall gate,** out of the forest, onto hummocky moorland with a view of isolated buildings at **Corryfoyness,** which was once a farm. There are boggy hollows spiked with rushes, as well as heathery humps, and some parts of the moorland are dotted with birch

A footbridge is crossed in a densely planted forest on the way from Drumnadrochit to Abriachan.

trees. The track meanders and climbs gradually to a **gateway** into another forest.

Signs inform visitors that this forest is managed by the Abriachan Forest Trust, and there are leaflets available detailing the Abriachan Forest Walks. The Great Glen Way is waymarked as usual, but signposts also point back to Drumnadrochit and ahead to Inverness. The track meanders and reaches the highest point on the entire route, around 380m (1245ft). There is a fairly steep descent to a building near **Achpopuli,** then the track swings right and leads straight down along a broad forest ride. The track is part of an old **drove road,** and towards the end there is access on the right to a **car park** and a grass-roofed toilet block, along with plenty of information about the Abriachan Forest Walks.

ABRIACHAN FOREST

Abriachan is only a small community of around 120 people, yet in the mid-1990s they managed to raise over £150,000 to buy a substantial part of the Abriachan Forest. At the time, it was the largest community forest in Scotland, and it has been developed with public access and conservation foremost. A network of walking and cycling trails has been established, as well as a car park complete with a picnic site, an eco-toilet and plenty of information. Interesting features just off the course of the Great Glen Way include Loch Laide and the Caiplich Prehistoric Settlement. Visitors who would like to support the work of the community can become Friends of the Abriachan Forest Trust, and receive a newsletter keeping them in touch with developments. Pick up a leaflet in the forest or check the website **www.abriachan.org.uk** for full contact details.

Keep straight ahead and the track leaves the forest, with a view of little **Loch Laide** to the right. Cross a minor road and go through a kissing gate to follow a narrow, but clear and obvious **gravel path.** This path rises gently up a moorland slope dotted with trees, meandering and clipping the corner of a **forest.** A sign points to the right towards a basic **campsite** just off-route. As the path approaches the whitewashed house of **Woodend,** it turns right and runs up to a kissing gate and a minor road, next to a sign for **Caiplich Farm.**

Turn left and follow the road through a forest, where there are a couple of

N–S route cont. p.83

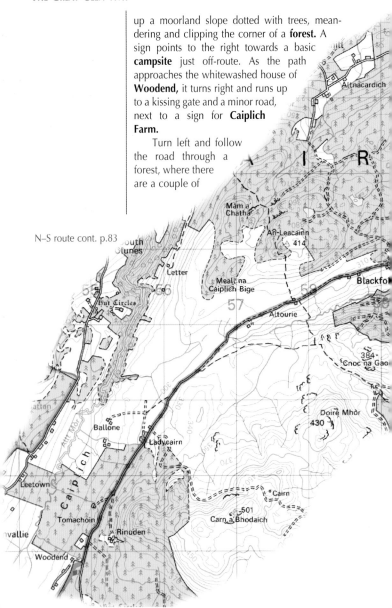

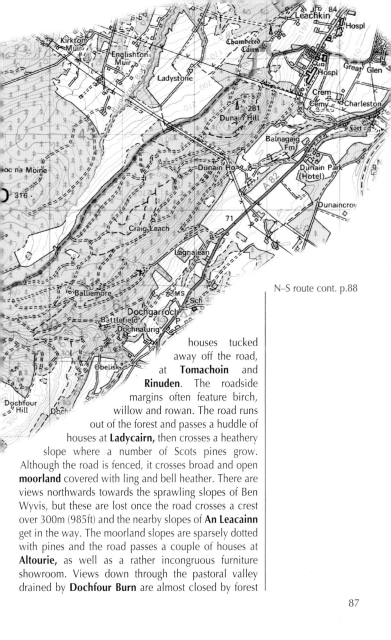

N–S route cont. p.88

houses tucked away off the road, at **Tomachoin** and **Rinuden**. The roadside margins often feature birch, willow and rowan. The road runs out of the forest and passes a huddle of houses at **Ladycairn,** then crosses a heathery slope where a number of Scots pines grow. Although the road is fenced, it crosses broad and open **moorland** covered with ling and bell heather. There are views northwards towards the sprawling slopes of Ben Wyvis, but these are lost once the road crosses a crest over 300m (985ft) and the nearby slopes of **An Leacainn** get in the way. The moorland slopes are sparsely dotted with pines and the road passes a couple of houses at **Altourie,** as well as a rather incongruous furniture showroom. Views down through the pastoral valley drained by **Dochfour Burn** are almost closed by forest

A lek is a site where rare black grouse traditionally gather at dawn during spring and autumn to perform noisy courtship displays. As a consequence, dogs should be kept under control.

plantations, but reveal a glimpse of the Great Glen and the countryside beyond. Continue along the minor road to reach a cottage at **Blackfold.**

Turn left as signposted along a **track,** then quickly turn right as marked through a **kissing gate,** into tall forest with no views. A sign reminds walkers that they are still following an old **drove road,** where cattle were driven from west to east, from the Highlands to Inverness. The route passes through ancient pinewoods that are being regenerated, and the sign also draws the attention of walkers to a nearby 'lek'. ◀

Follow the **track** into the forest and turn left at a junction to stay on the main track. The forest floor is grassy, heathery and mossy, with areas of bilberry. The track meanders and undulates slightly, passing another **kissing gate** before heading more noticeably downhill. Old drystone walls flank the drove road and the **ruin** of an old 'lairage', once used as a lodging by drovers, is passed just before a couple of prominent horse chestnut trees.

Moss, heather and bilberry grow thick on top of the flanking walls, and plenty of slender birch and rowan trees grow alongside, often obscuring the ranks of conifers beyond. After passing beneath **power lines,** look out to the right to spot some fine examples of Scots pines, and also look to the left, between the birch trees, to glimpse the waters of the Beauly Firth; a sure sign that this walk across Scotland is drawing to a conclusion.

Go through a **kissing gate** and follow a broader track downhill, but turn right at a track junction to pass a **pylon** and go through an **old gateway.** Walk out of the woods, through a **kissing gate** on the left, and cross a dam holding a **pond** in place. There is a view of Inverness in the distance, then as the path climbs up a grassy slope, there are fine views of the stone-built Creag Dunain hospital closer to hand. The path runs down a grassy slope and bends to the right to reach a **kissing gate.** Turn left down a track, passing a variety of trees, including stout beech and towering Scots pines. The track is grassy as it bends right to a **kissing gate** to reach a road and a Great Glen Way signpost in the grounds of **Creag Dunain.**

The course of an old drovers' road is followed through a remnant Scots pine forest beyond Blackfold.

CREAG DUNAIN HOSPITAL

Built in 1864, Creag Dunain was originally a huge Victorian mental hospital. By all accounts, its management was progressive and doctors were willing to practise the latest forms of treatment on their patients. The building was later used as a general hospital, and more recently the site has been expanded with the addition of modern annexes, so that the Great Glen Way is obliged to weave its way between its buildings on its way into the city.

Turn left down the road as marked, then left, right and left again to pass a small gate-lodge building and **bus stop.** Turn right as signposted for the Great Glen Way and follow markers through the hospital grounds to pick

N–S route cont. p.86

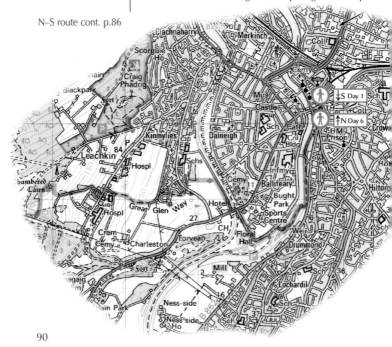

up a clear **gravel path** winding downhill between fields, with rampant hedgerows alongside. The path swings left beside some **houses,** then there is a right turn down through a broad and **grassy space** between houses. Cross a road to go through another grassy space, and drift left as marked to cross a **road-end** and go through an **underpass** beneath a busy road with bus stops.

Follow a **paved path,** then turn right alongside a golf course and follow a path along an **embankment** between the golf course and sports pitches. Steps lead up to the **Caledonian Canal.** Turn right to follow a tarmac track parallel, bearing in mind that this is actually running roughly in the direction of Fort William! Turn left across a **swing bridge** on the busy A82 road, then cross with care. There are buses along this road, as well as the Hebrides bed and breakfast.

A glimpse of the splendid stone towers and turrets of the Creag Dunain Hospital on the outskirts of Inverness.

Several splendid suspension foot- bridges span the powerful flow of the River Ness throughout Inverness.

Do not follow the canal path, or the road running parallel, but follow the path marked as the Great Glen Way, running parallel to the road. Head diagonally left through the car park of the **Inverness Sports Centre,** then turn right at the **Floral Hall** and coffee shop. Turn left to walk alongside another road, crossing over it to keep left of a toilet block near **Whin Park.**

Turn left as marked along a tarmac path, then when the path runs alongside the **River Ness,** turn right to cross a white suspension footbridge onto the **Ness Islands.** Turn left alongside the river again, then turn right across a **curved footbridge,** which has a small island in its middle. Keep right along another path, then when the island tapers out, turn right across another **suspension footbridge.** Turn left to walk alongside the **River Ness,** but turn right later to cross a short **foot- bridge** over a narrow water channel running parallel.

Turn left alongside the river and follow it into **Inverness.** The popular path is known as **Ladies' Walk** as far as a suspension footbridge, then it becomes **Ness Bank.** Watch out for a right turn away from the river, along an alley beside **Ness Bank House.** Climb up a few steps and turn left up the road called **View Bank** to reach **Inverness Castle.**

INVERNESS CASTLE

Castle Hill rises proudly above the River Ness and is obviously a strategic location. It may have been settled and fortified throughout history, but there was certainly a timber fort there in the 11th century. A stone fort was built in the 12th century, which was rebuilt in the 15th century. The castle was extensively damaged at the end of the Jacobite Rebellion in 1746. The neo-Norman castle seen today, of well-dressed red sandstone, was built in 1834 as the Sheriff Court. It remains a Sheriff Court and only the Drum Tower can be visited, where the Castle Garrison Encounter is open on a limited basis. Outside the castle a statue of Flora MacDonald gazes towards the Great Glen. She was imprisoned in London for helping Bonnie Prince Charlie.

The Great Glen Way finishes at a stone **monument** overlooking the River Ness and the later stages of the route. Spend a while looking back towards the Great Glen, then give some thought to how you will spend your remaining time in **Inverness.**

Behind Inverness Castle is the **Castle Wynd,** which leads down past toilets to the Tourist Information Centre and the **High Street.** Walkers will naturally find themselves exploring at least a small part of the city centre, even if they only want to head for the train or bus station. Those who stay overnight will have more time at their disposal and can enjoy further explorations of the city. (See the next section for a brief description of Inverness.)

View across the River Ness from Inverness Castle to St Andrew's Cathedral at the start of the Great Glen Way (Day 1 N–S)

INVERNESS

The origins of Inverness stretch back some 7000 years, and while Inverness Castle is basically an 18th-century edifice, it occupies a strategic site that has been fortified throughout the millennia. In the AD565 St Columba visited the Pictish king Brude nearby. Shakespeare had Macbeth murder Duncan here in the 11th century, but the play is not a true record of history. Inverness was made a royal burgh in the 12th century and granted several charters, quickly establishing itself as a centre for trading and shipbuilding. The first bridge over the powerful River Ness was built in the 13th century, and a Dominican Friary was established.

Centuries of Highland strife saw Inverness suffer a succession of attacks and burnings, with peaceful interludes allowing for rebuilding, and its story throughout the Middle Ages was one of slow growth and increasing prosperity. When Cromwellian troops occupied Inverness in the middle of the 17th century, they built a garrison, of which only one tower survives. Jacobites occupied the castle in 1746, leaving it in ruins. Following the Rebellion, a huge fortified barracks was constructed outside the town, known as Fort George. Inverness continued to expand, and wooden buildings with thatched roofs were gradually replaced by more substantial stone structures. The town developed a thriving port and gained several splendid buildings and new industries. While bridges over the River Ness proliferated, the Kessock Bridge between the Moray and Beauly Firth dates only from 1982. In the year 2000, Inverness was granted city status to take it into the 21st century. The city proudly proclaims itself as the 'Capital of the Highlands'.

Facilities around Inverness include plenty of accommodation, including a campsite and youth hostel, both handy for the city centre. There are banks with ATMs, post offices, toilets, plenty of pubs, restaurants, cafés and take-aways. There are also shops of all types, including gift shops and outdoor equipment shops. The Inverness Museum and Art Gallery is on Castle Wynd, below the castle, and the Tourist Information Office is in the same building (☎01463-234353, email inverness@host.co.uk). Those who wish to embark on a town trail can obtain information here, as well as information about services and attractions throughout the city and surrounding area.

There are plenty of bus services around Inverness, as well as into the surrounding countryside and further afield. There are also rail services, as well as a nearby airport.

A statue of Flora MacDonald looks back along the course of the Great Glen Way from Inverness Castle.

DAY 1

Inverness to Drumnadrochit

Start	Inverness Castle – grid ref 666451
Finish	Tourist Information Centre, Drumnadrochit – grid ref 507299
Distance	29km (18 miles)
Total Ascent	540m (1770ft)
Maps	OS Landranger 26, OS Explorer 416N Harvey Great Glen Way
Terrain	Urban pathways through green spaces, followed by forest paths and tracks. A long road walk, followed by forest and moorland tracks. A road walk to finish.
Refreshments	Inverness and Drumnadrochit.
Public Transport	Local city bus services around Inverness. Regular daily Scottish Citylink buses link Inverness with Drumnadrochit and Fort William.

This is the longest day's walk on the Great Glen Way, and there is a fine view from Inverness Castle towards the Great Glen. Take care over route-finding through the city suburbs, where one green space after another is linked to provide a route to the countryside. The route actually drifts away from the Great Glen, following the course of an old drove road through an interesting remnant Scots pine forest. A road-walk leads to the Abriachan Forest, which is managed by the local community, who have cleared, marked and signposted a network of trails. The area is proving popular with visitors and school parties, and the highest point on the Great Glen Way is crossed around 380m (1245ft). Drumnadrochit is reached at the end of the day, where the principal attractions are two rival exhibitions devoted to Loch Ness and its 'monster'.

Walkers starting at either the railway station or bus station in **Inverness** will have to negotiate the busy city streets for a few minutes to find **Inverness Castle.** This is prominently located on a green hill just behind the Town House and Tourist Information Centre, overlooking the

For map, see pp. 81–93

Inverness Castle, built of striking red sandstone, crowns a grassy hill in the very heart of Inverness.

powerful flow of the River Ness. A **stone monument** marks the start of the Great Glen Way, and the route is marked throughout with signs bearing a 'thistle' logo. A statue of Flora MacDonald gazes along the length of the Great Glen.

INVERNESS CASTLE

Castle Hill rises proudly above the River Ness and is obviously a strategic location. It may have been settled and fortified throughout history, but there was certainly a timber fort there in the 11th century. A stone fort was built in the 12th century, which was rebuilt in the 15th century. The castle was extensively damaged at the end of the Jacobite Rebellion in 1746. The neo-Norman castle seen today, of well-dressed red sandstone, was built in 1834 as the Sheriff Court. It remains a Sheriff Court and only the Drum Tower can be visited, where the Castle Garrison Encounter is open on a limited basis.

Walk down the road called **View Bank,** and cross a busy road to continue straight ahead. Almost immediately, turn right down some stone steps and walk through an alley beside **Ness Bank House,** to reach the **River Ness.** Turn left to walk along a popular riverside path, called **Ness Bank,** until it reaches a white suspension footbridge, where it becomes **Ladies' Walk.** Continue beside the river, then cross a short **footbridge** on the right, which spans a narrow water channel, then turn left to walk along a path between the channel and the river. Turn right to cross a suspension footbridge onto the **Ness Islands,** then turn left and keep left. Later, cross a **curved footbridge,** which has a small island in its middle, and turn left to walk alongside the river again. Turn right to cross another **suspension footbridge,** then turn left to follow the river, and a narrow channel, to a toilet block near **Whin Park.**

Cross over a **road** and look for a path running parallel to it, to reach a nearby road junction. Turn right to reach the **Floral Hall** and coffee shop, then turn left and walk diagonally left through the car park of the **Inverness Sports Centre.** Look for markers to find another path running parallel to a road, then turn left at the Hebrides bed and breakfast to follow the busy A82 road across a **swing bridge** on the **Caledonian Canal.** The road has bus services.

Turn right to follow a clear tarmac track beside the canal, which actually leads back towards Inverness! However, there are **steps** down to the left, leading onto a path following an **embankment** between a golf course and sports pitches. Keep straight ahead and later turn left along a **paved path,** which goes through an **underpass** beneath a busy road with bus stops.

Walk past a **road-end,** then drift right across a grassy area as marked, looking for a **grassy space** between houses. Cross a road and walk gently up through another broader grassy space between houses. Turn left along a path behind some **houses,** then drift right as marked to follow a clear **gravel path** winding uphill between fields, with rampant hedgerows alongside. Follow the markers through the grounds of **Creag Dunain Hospital,** turning left along a road to reach a **bus stop** and a small lodge building. Turn right, left, and right again as marked, to find the Great Glen Way signposted on the right at the edge of the hospital grounds. The fiddly route-finding through the suburbs of Inverness is over, and ahead lies more open countryside.

CREAG DUNAIN HOSPITAL

Built in 1864, Creag Dunain was originally a huge Victorian mental hospital. By all accounts, its management was progressive and doctors were willing to practise the latest forms of treatment on their patients. The building was later used as a general hospital, and more recently the site has been expanded with the addition of modern annexes, so that the Great Glen Way is obliged to weave its way between its buildings on its way out of the city.

Go through a **kissing gate** and follow a clear, grassy track as it bends left uphill. It passes a variety of trees, including towering Scots pines and stout beech. Turn right through another **kissing gate** and follow a clear path uphill. It bends to the left and runs up across a grassy slope, enjoying fine views of the stone-built hospital below. Follow the path down another grassy slope and look back towards Inverness, which will soon be lost to view. Cross a dam holding a **pond** in place, go through a **kissing gate** and turn right along a woodland track. Go through an **old gateway** and past a **pylon,** then turn left up a broader track. Go through a **kissing gate** onto yet another track.

A sign reminds walkers that they are following an old **drove road,** where cattle were driven from west to east, from the Highlands to Inverness. The route passes through ancient pinewoods that are being regenerated, and the sign also draws the attention of walkers to a nearby 'lek'. ▶ Look out to the left to spot Scots pines, and to the right, between birch trees, to glimpse the waters of the Beauly Firth.

A lek is a site where rare black grouse traditionally gather at dawn during spring and autumn to perform noisy courtship displays. As a consequence, dogs should be kept under control.

Pass under **power lines** and note how plenty of slender birch and rowan trees grow alongside, often obscuring the ranks of conifers beyond. Moss, heather and bilberry grow thick on top of the old **drystone walls** that flank the track. Just after passing a couple of prominent chestnut trees, the **ruin** of an old 'lairage' is passed, which was once used by drovers. The track rises to a **kissing gate,** then meanders and undulates slightly without its flanking drystone walls. The forest floor is grassy, heathery and mossy, with areas of bilberry. Turn right at a **junction** to stay on the main track, and eventually go through a final **kissing gate** where views begin to open up. Turn left to reach a minor road at a cottage at **Blackfold.**

Turn right along the road, as signposted for the Great Glen Way. Views down through the pastoral valley drained by **Dochfour Burn** are almost closed by forest plantations, but reveal a glimpse of the Great Glen and the countryside beyond. The slopes of **An Leacainn,** up to the right, are sparsely dotted with pines and the road passes a rather incongruous furniture showroom and a

A remnant Scots pine forest sprawls across a heather moorland frequented by black grouse near Blackfold.

couple of houses at **Altourie.** Although the road is fenced, it crosses a broad **moorland** covered with ling and bell heather, then when it crosses a crest over 300m (985ft), there are views northwards towards the sprawling slopes of Ben Wyvis. After crossing a heathery slope where a number of Scots pines grow, the road passes a huddle of houses at **Ladycairn.** ▶ Watch out for a sign for **Caiplich Farm,** and go through a kissing gate on the right to leave the road.

A clear and obvious **gravel path** runs downhill and swings left in view of a white house called **Woodend.** Later, a sign points left for a basic **campsite,** just off-route. The path clips the corner of a **forest** and descends gently down a moorland slope dotted with trees, meandering before running straight to a **kissing gate** onto a minor road. Walk straight ahead along a forest track, with a view of little **Loch Laide** to the left. Also to the left, a little later, is access to a car park and a grass-roofed toilet block, along with plenty of information about the Abriachan Forest Walks.

The roadside margins often feature birch, willow and rowan on the way through a forest, and there are a couple of houses tucked away off the road, at **Tomachoin** and **Rinuden.**

ABRIACHAN FOREST

Abriachan is only a small community of around 120 people, yet in the mid-1990s they managed to raise over £150,000 to buy a substantial part of the Abriachan Forest. At the time, it was the largest community forest in Scotland, and it has been developed with public access and conservation foremost. A network of walking and cycling trails has been established, as well as a car park complete with a picnic site, an eco-toilet and plenty of information. Interesting features just off the course of the Great Glen Way include Loch Laide and the Caiplich Prehistoric Settlement. Visitors who would like to support the work of the community can become Friends of the Abriachan Forest Trust, and receive a newsletter keeping them in touch with developments. Pick up a leaflet in the forest or check the website **www.abriachan.org.uk** for full contact details.

The Great Glen Way is waymarked as usual, but signposts also point back to Inverness and ahead to Drumnadrochit. The track is still part of the old **drove road** that was followed earlier, and it leads straight up along a broad forest ride. Swing left to pass a building near **Achpopuli** and climb fairly steeply, levelling out on the highest point on the entire route, around 380m (1245ft). The track meanders gently downhill and leaves the forest at a **gateway.**

Continue meandering gently downhill on a moorland slope dotted with birch trees. There are boggy hollows spiked with rushes, as well as heathery humps, and there is a view of isolated buildings at **Corryfoyness.** Go through a **tall gate** into another forest, following a track that gradually moves closer towards Loch Ness. The first views over the loch are not particularly good, as the track descends gradually on a clear-felled slope. Views are lost as the track undulates, then suddenly gives way to a **forest path.**

The path runs downhill a short way, then crosses **stepping stones** over a small burn. Follow the path uphill, then downhill, then continue more or less level for a while. After passing through a more open area of grass and bracken, with several birch trees growing, the path turns sharply left and right downhill. The path enters dense forest with no views, and little light reaches the forest floor, so only moss and wood sorrel grow alongside. Descend gradually to cross a **footbridge,** then there is a glimpse of Loch Ness before the path reaches a **gate** at the edge of the forest.

Follow the path across a **grassy slope** overlooking a stretch of Loch Ness, now featuring a view of Urquhart Castle. The path climbs through small gates, then enters woods and crosses a narrow access road that leads to **Tychat.** The path drops through more small gates and runs parallel to the main **A82 road.** There is another brief glimpse of Urquhart Castle across Urquhart Bay on Loch Ness. Follow a path around a tall fence to pass **Temple House,** then go down through a gate and follow the access road down to the main road. There is access on

There is a view across Urquhart Bay on Loch Ness on the final descent towards the village of Drumnadrochit.

the other side of the road for **Urquhart Bay Harbour,** for cruises on Loch Ness. Turn right to follow the main road, keeping to the pavement on the right-hand side throughout, passing a handful of bed and breakfast places to reach **Drumnadrochit.**

LOCH NESS

Walkers will seldom be able to see the whole of Loch Ness, but will often catch a glimpse of some part of it. The deep trough it occupies has been filled with water ever since the end of the last Ice Age around 10,000 years ago, and it reflects enough light to brighten even the dullest days in the Great Glen. Six major rivers carry water into Loch Ness, from a part of the Highlands known for high rainfall, explaining why the River Ness flows so powerfully past Inverness. Here are some facts and figures to help appreciate its full extent:

- Catchment area – 1800 square kilometres (700 square miles)
- Surface area – 56 square kilometres (22 square miles)
- Length – 37 kilometres (23 miles)
- Width – 3 kilometres (1.9 miles)
- Shoreline length – 86 kilometres (53.5 miles)
- Volume – 7.5 cubic kilometres (1.8 cubic miles)
- Maximum depth – 230m (755ft)
- Surface level – 16m (52ft) above sea level

There is only one island in Loch Ness, the diminutive Cherry Island near Fort Augustus, which is actually an ancient man-made island dwelling, or crannog. More astonishing facts include oft-repeated statements that the volume of water in the loch exceeds that of all the lakes and reservoirs in England and Wales, and is sufficient to immerse the entire population of the world!

DRUMNADROCHIT

Drumnadrochit (*Gaelic* – Druim na Drochaid) is a busy little village with plenty to catch the attention of passing tourists. Two attractions vying for attention are the 'Original' Loch Ness Monster Visitor Centre, at the Loch Ness Lodge Hotel, open all year (☎01456-450432), and the 'Official' Loch Ness 2000 Exhibition, at the Drumnadrochit Hotel, open all year (☎01456-450573). There are entrance charges to both places. Whatever you want to know about Loch Ness and its 'monster', this is the place to take on board all the opinions, then you can make up your own mind. If nothing more than a 'Nessie' souvenir is required, a handful of gift shops around the village deal in the widest selection of products.

There is accommodation to suit every pocket, from hotels to guest houses and bed and breakfast places, with an independent hostel in Lewiston and a campsite further along the road at Borlum. Most facilities are clustered round the village green at Drumnadrochit. There is a bank with an ATM, a post office store, toilets, bars, restaurants, cafés and takeaways. There are souvenir and gift shops, as well as a Tourist Information Centre (☎01456-459050). Regular daily Scottish Citylink buses link Drumnadrochit with Inverness and Fort William. Cruises on Loch Ness are also available.

DAY 2

Drumnadrochit to Invermoriston

Start	Tourist Information Centre, Drumnadrochit – grid ref 507299
Finish	Glenmoriston Arms Hotel, Invermoriston – grid ref 420168
Distance	23km (14 miles)
Total Ascent	590m (1935ft)
Maps	OS Landrangers 26 & 34, OS Explorer 416S, Harvey Great Glen Way
Terrain	A moorland road, followed by forest paths and tracks.
Refreshments	Plenty of restaurants, cafés and take-aways in Drumnadrochit. Hotel-restaurant and coffee shop at Invermoriston.
Public Transport	Regular daily Scottish Citylink buses link Drumnadrochit and Invermoriston with Fort William and Inverness, and these services can also be accessed at Loch Ness Youth Hostel at Alltsigh.

On leaving Drumnadrochit, walkers have to decide whether to make a detour to visit Urquhart Castle. Those who can't spare the time can console themselves by studying a floral model of the castle in the middle of the village green in Drumnadrochit. The Great Glen Way climbs from the village and follows a moorland road to Balbeg. Later, while following forest tracks, there are extensive views along the length of Loch Ness. After a descent to Alltsigh, the route climbs uphill and a viewpoint can be reached by a short diversion. This offers a glimpse of what the landscape looked like before commercial forests were planted. Invermoriston is a tiny village and is quickly explored in the evening. If planning to stay there, it is wise to book lodgings in advance, although it is a simple matter to catch a bus elsewhere in search of accommodation.

For map, see pp. 70–80

Follow the busy A82 road out of **Drumnadrochit.** The road bends right, then left to reach the neighbouring village of **Lewiston,** which has a small range of facilities. Cross the River Coiltie and turn right at a picnic area, as signposted for the Clunebeg Estate. Alternatively follow the path beside the main road, straight ahead to visit **Urquhart Castle**, then return to this junction later.

URQUHART CASTLE

Urquhart Castle is 2km (1.25 miles) off-route, or 3.25km (2 miles) from Drumnadrochit, perched on Stone Point overlooking Loch Ness. It can be reached safely on foot as there is a path beside the busy A82 road, and Scottish Citylink buses serve both Drumnadrochit and the castle. The situation is splendid and it is a renowned place for those keeping a lookout for the Loch Ness Monster! Once one of the largest castles in Scotland, Urquhart Castle's sprawling ruins take time to explore. A visitor centre offers a thorough grounding in its construction and history, plus a café. Urquhart Castle is open all year and there is an entrance charge (☎01456-450551).

A Bronze Age promontory fort once stood on Stone Point, and there were other defensive structures on the site before Urquhart Castle was built in the 13th century. Its history is one of intense conflict, in which English and Scots alternately occupied it,

The tower house at Urquhart Castle is a popular place for visitors to keep a lookout for the Loch Ness 'monster'.

with William Wallace and Robert the Bruce each holding the property for a time. Buchan, son of Robert II, held the castle from 1390, ruling with brutal force, and frequently robbing churches. In the 15th and 16th centuries the MacDonalds launched raids on the castle, which was later held by the Grants. The bulk of the damage to the castle was done with explosives in 1692, which prevented it becoming a Jacobite stronghold in subsequent years.

Visitors cross a wooden gangway across a defensive ditch, and pass through a gatehouse. However, in the past, most people approaching the castle would have done so through a watergate from Loch Ness. The centrepiece of Urquhart Castle is a stout and impressive tower house, but be sure to take note of the complex arrangement of the ruined defensive walls that surround the site. The best vantage point is of course from the top of the tower house.

Follow the minor road straight ahead to reach a big sign for the **Clunebeg Estate,** and continue walking straight ahead along a clear track. Although the track runs level alongside the bouldery **River Coiltie,** a variety of densely packed trees usually screen the river from view. Any houses seen on the far side are part of the village of **Lewiston.** Admire tall oaks and beech trees while following the track up to **Clunebeg House** and follow a waymarked path straight ahead from **Clunebeg Lodge.** The path swings left as it climbs across a slope of fine oaks and bracken, and there are views back towards Drumnadrochit. Go through a **gate** and cross a footbridge to enter a dense forest, where there is later a brief glimpse of Drumnadrochit to the left. The path turns right and runs up to a gate on a track, where a left turn leads quickly up to another gate and a **minor road.**

Turn right as signposted for the Great Glen Way, climbing steeply up past a house called **Woodend.** The road climbs at a gentler gradient and later leaves the forest. A **path** runs parallel, off to the right, as the road undulates across **heather moorland** around 250m (820ft).

The road has to be followed again, and a swathe of rough grassland lies to the left, while improved pasture lies to the right. Gorse grows on either side of the road as it descends a boggy moorland slope, later passing the **Ancarraig Lodges.** Look ahead to see the humped hills of Meall Fuar-mhonaidh and Creag Dhearg. There are occasional glimpses of Loch Ness while passing isolated houses and farms. Use another path running parallel to the road around **Balbeg,** finally dropping down into a **car park.** The road continues to a nearby pottery, but the Great Glen Way turns left through a **gate.**

Follow a track downhill from the road, generally downstream alongside **Grotaig Burn,** and go through another gate. Cross over the burn and climb a short way to reach a gate on a **grassy gap** below the wooded knoll bearing the remains of an ancient fort called **Dùn Scriben.** There is a view of a tiny portion of Loch Ness. Go through the gate and follow the track downhill among tall oaks, swinging right at the bottom to go through another **gate** in a deer fence. A clear path descends, which can be a little rugged in places, and may be muddy when wet. It is fringed with young birch trees and drops onto a **forest track.** Turn right to follow the track uphill, and watch out for an opening in the trees on the left, where there is a view north-east along Loch Ness. There is generally a grassy strip along the middle of the track, and it climbs quite steeply before making a slight descent. Continue straight onwards to reach a **turning space.**

Continue along a **narrow path,** which is rough and stony in places and may be muddy in parts when wet. The trees alongside the path diminish in height, giving way to younger forest trees, a few tall birch and scrubby slopes of bracken, broom and heather. There are views directly across Loch Ness to the village of Foyers, then the path suddenly reaches another **turning space** at the end of a forest track. Follow the track gently uphill, losing the views as the trees grow taller. There is often a grassy strip along the middle then it crosses a concrete bridge over the **Allt Ghiubhnais.** The track undulates close to 300m (985ft) above **Ruskich Wood.**

Looking ahead through the Great Glen from a high-level forest track. Loch Oich is just visible in the far distance.

The tall trees give way to clear-felled slopes that are profusely covered in rosebay willowherb. Views along the Great Glen are very good, especially from a **sharp left bend,** stretching far beyond Fort Augustus to reveal a glimpse of Loch Oich. Looking far across Loch Ness, the remote Monadh Liath range rolls southwards into the distance. Take the sharp left bend, later followed by a sharp right bend, to descend and enjoy more of the same views. The track later bends quickly left and right again to descend further.

There is another sharp left bend and sharp right bend above **Primrose Bay,** then views along the Great Glen are later lost as the track descends among tall conifers. Simply keep walking downhill, but note that there is an exit to the left leading to the Briarbank bed and breakfast, before another track junction is reached at **Alltsigh.**

ALLTSIGH

A sign simply states SYHA and points down a track and through a gate. The track passes a white house and quickly reaches the busy A82 road beside Loch

Ness. Immediately to the left is Briarbank bed and breakfast, while further away to the right is Loch Ness Youth Hostel and a bus stop. The hostel occupies a site offering splendid views across the loch.

Those who don't need to detour to **Alltsigh** can simply walk straight along a **forest track** as marked, crossing a concrete bridge over a rocky gorge. There is a waterfall in the gorge, as well as a fine variety of trees, while a diligent search reveals an old packhorse bridge. Climb steeply uphill, passing a **junction of tracks,** then walk further uphill, downhill, and gently uphill along a track fringed with broom. Keep straight ahead at a **junction of tracks** beside a rock cutting, descending gently for a while. The track passes a slope of gorse bushes where no forest trees were ever planted. A bend is reached where there is a good **viewpoint** revealing the length of Loch Ness, but also turn and admire the fine variety of trees stacked against the cliffs of **Creag nan Eun.** Later, while climbing uphill, a post draws attention to the **Stone**

A view of Loch Ness from the rugged garden in front of Loch Ness Youth Hostel at Alltsigh.

The Stone Cave is located beside a forest track on the way from Alltsigh towards Invermoriston.

Cave, said to have been built to offer shelter to a washerwoman on her frequent journeys between Alltsigh and Invermoriston. It still offers splendid shelter. Follow the track further uphill at a gentle gradient, with occasional glimpses of Loch Ness, then turn right to follow a narrow and bendy **forest path** uphill as marked, to reach another **forest track** at a higher level.

Turn left to follow the track, then turn left at a nearby junction as marked, but also consider turning right as signposted for a nearby viewpoint. This short detour reveals a narrow path winding up a slope covered in ling and bell heather to reach the crude **Stone Seat,** where there is a fine view over Loch Ness. The village of Invermoriston, despite being close at hand, is completely hidden from view. Retrace your steps to the junction. Follow the track uphill to another junction, then turn left and go through a tall **gateway.** Follow the track across a concrete bridge over the **Allt Coinneag.** The track swings left, then right, then while crossing a crest, a thinner part of the plantation reveals some of the former heather cover and low rocky outcrops. The track makes a gentle descent among closely packed trees, to cross a bridge over a stream and reach a **minor road.**

Turn left to follow the road across a bridge over the same stream, and simply walk downhill among densely packed conifers. The steep and narrow road zigzags down a well-wooded slope bearing birch, oak, beech and sycamore, with a holly understorey. The road lands on the **A887 road,** where a left turn leads past the **Clog & Craft Shop** and a milestone warns 'Last Clog Shop before Skye – 52 miles'. Walk straight into Invermoriston.

INVERMORISTON

Invermoriston (*Gaelic* – Inbhir Mor Eason) has only a few facilities, but at the end of the day these prove most welcome. The Glenmoriston Arms Hotel is very prominent. It was originally a drovers' inn, dating from 1740, and the oldest parts are around the bar and reception area. Johnson and Boswell stayed there while planning a trip to the Hebrides in 1773. There are a few bed and breakfast places in and around the village, as well as the Glenmoriston Stores Post Office, Pig's Nose Coffee Shop and Restaurant, and the Clog and Craft Shop. Toilets are available inside the Glenmoriston Millennium Hall, when open. Regular daily Scottish Citylink buses link Invermoriston with Fort William and Inverness, as well as the Isle of Skye.

THE SEVEN MEN OF GLEN MORISTON

The date was July 27th 1746, when Bonnie Prince Charlie was on the run after the crushing defeat at the Battle of Culloden. Pursued by 'Butcher' Cumberland, and with a bounty of £30,000 on his head, Charles had not eaten for two days and was clad in rags by the time he reached Glen Moriston. Coming upon a crude hut and ravenously hungry, he was warned by his companions not to seek food or shelter in case he was recognised. Charles declared 'I had better be killed like a man than starved like a fool', and made his way to the hut. The seven men inside were mere outlaws, and one of them recognised him, but to their credit, they spurned the chance to claim the bounty and risked their lives to feed and shelter him. Meanwhile, on the road through Glen Moriston, an Edinburgh merchant named Roderick MacKenzie, who bore a passing resemblance to the Bonnie Prince, was shot at by troops. As he died he declared, 'Alas, you have killed your prince', and this ruse was sufficient to buy enough time for Charles to be smuggled out of the country.

DAY 3

Invermoriston to Fort Augustus

Start	Glenmoriston Arms Hotel, Invermoriston – grid ref 420168
Finish	Fort Augustus Swing Bridge – grid ref 379092
Distance	13km (8 miles)
Total Ascent	320m (1050ft)
Maps	OS Landranger 34, OS Explorer 416S, Harvey Great Glen Way
Terrain	Forest tracks and paths with some short, steep slopes.
Refreshments	Invermoriston has a hotel with a bar-restaurant and one other restaurant. There are plenty of bars, restaurants, cafés and take-aways around Fort Augustus.
Public Transport	Regular daily Scottish Citylink buses link Invermoriston and Fort Augustus with Fort William and Inverness. The Loch Ness Express ferry links Fort Augustus with Dochgarroch, near Inverness.

This is a very short day's walk; indeed, it could easily be covered in a morning or an afternoon, and some walkers simply add it to the following day's walk if they are trying to complete the Great Glen Way in a hurry. This short day's walk could allow walkers a whole afternoon to explore Fort Augustus, maybe including a cruise on Loch Ness in order to gain a greater appreciation of its vastness. While the Great Glen Way often runs close to Loch Ness, forested slopes often shield it from view, so walkers see less of it than they might imagine. The bustling village of Fort Augustus has several points of interest and it is well worth discovering some of them in the evening.

Leave **Invermoriston** by following the main A82 road downhill to cross the River Moriston, then turn right along a minor road. However, note the ravaged remains of **Telford's Bridge** spanning the River Moriston, and the splendid Moriston Falls that spill beneath it.

For map, see pp. 63–69

The Old Bridge, or Telford's Bridge, is slowly crumbling away and can be viewed from the nearby road bridge.

TELFORD'S BRIDGE

The ramshackle remains of Telford's Bridge, also known as the Old Bridge, could be crossed in preference to the main road bridge, but take care as the masonry is in a bad state of repair. Despite being nothing more than a standard double-span stone arch, its construction spanned several years from 1805 until 1813, owing to a 'languid and inattentive contractor' and 'idle workers'. The bridge is one of more than a thousand associated with Telford.

The minor road passes the wooden **Dalcataig Chalets,** and is mostly wooded as it rises and falls gently. The tarmac expires as the road reaches a few houses at **Dalcataig.** Turn left as marked up a steep and stony **path** to reach a **track** at a higher level. Turn left steeply up the track and pass a **rocky outcrop.** The track, however, climbs and later descends. Birch and alder often screen the coniferous forest on the next ascent, and there is a glimpse of the village of Invermoriston down to the left, which is actually quite close. The track enjoys a brief view of Loch Ness as it swings right to leave **Glen Moriston,** crossing over a crest and running downhill.

A broader track is reached on a sharp bend, so keep straight ahead to climb steeply uphill. ▶ The gradient eases and there are eventually good views of Loch Ness from a clear-felled slope. A gentle descent leads across a concrete bridge over a small **waterfall,** losing the views and crossing a dip in the track. Cross a concrete bridge over **Portclair Burn,** climb gently, then there are more views across Loch Ness, taking in the hill of Beinn a' Bhacaidh rising from the far shore. Descend gently from a young part of the forest into tall forest, where a concrete bridge spans a waterfall on the **Allt a' Mhuilinn.** The track climbs over a gentle rise where there is a **stone-slab seat,** and views both ways along Loch Ness seem endless, as well as stretching across the loch to the rugged hill of Beinn a' Bhacaidh.

Follow the track downhill and uphill, enjoying good views over a slope of young trees. Descend gradually among tall trees and keep straight ahead at a **junction.** There is a slight dip in the track, then a descent among tall conifers, with margins of heather, bilberry, mosses, ferns and wood sorrel. Pass a **gate** and avoid a right turn as the track descends and bends. The lower woods are

Campers should walk down the main track in order to reach the Loch Ness Caravan and Camping Park at Rubha Bàn, with the minimum of walking along the A82.

A view of Loch Ness and Beinn a' Bhacaidh, seen from a forested slope on the way to Fort Augustus.

A view across the southern reaches of Loch Ness from a forested slope high above Allt na Criche.

mixed, with some fine oaks and birch, then the track swings left to cross a tumbling stream at **Allt na Criche,** almost reaching the busy main road.

Just before the main road, turn right through a **gate** and follow another track uphill. Plenty of birch trees grow among the conifers, and there are good views of the head of Loch Ness near Fort Augustus. Walk gently uphill and watch out for a turning on the left down a path. The steep slope is covered in tall, stately pines, then a **footbridge** is crossed in a wood at the bottom. A **riverside path** leads to a minor road, quite close to the main road, at **Three Bridges.**

Turn right to follow the narrow minor road uphill, passing a couple of bed and breakfast places. Keep straight ahead at a **junction.** ◀ The minor road running downhill is called **Bunoich Brae** and leads to the busy **A82 road,** but look out for a tarmac path making a short cut to the right before the junction. Turn right to follow the main road into **Fort Augustus,** passing the Tourist Information Centre and crossing a bridge over the River Oich to reach a swing bridge on the **Caledonian Canal.**

A right turn at the junction, for Jenkins Park and Auchterawe, leads to the Great Glen Way Rangers' base.

FORT AUGUSTUS

The earliest settlement at Fort Augustus (*Gaelic* – Cill Chuimein) was founded in the 6th century by monks from Iona, led by St Cumin. Precious little else is recorded about the place until, in the aftermath of the Jacobite Rising of 1715, a fort was constructed on the site now occupied by the Lovat Hotel. When General Wade built a military road through the area in 1726, the fort was moved to where the Abbey now stands. Fort Augustus was named after William Augustus, Duke of Cumberland, and was destroyed at the beginning of the Jacobite Rising of 1745. 'Butcher' Cumberland had it rebuilt while engaged in a brutal campaign to suppress the Highland clans. The site was given to the Benedictines in 1876, who built the Abbey, vacating it in 1997. The Abbey has since been redeveloped and there is no longer any public access to it.

A Great Glen Way marker post stands beside the Caledonian Canal on the way out of Fort Augustus.

121

The bustling tourist village of Fort Augustus is halfway along the Great Glen Way. It offers plenty of accommodation, from a campsite and humble bed and breakfast places to fine hotels. There is a bank, but if an ATM is needed, then go to the Spar shop. There is a post office and a choice of food and gift shops. There are several bars, restaurants, cafés and take-aways. Toilets are located beside the Tourist Information Centre (☎01320-366367). There are regular daily bus services to Fort William and Inverness. Cruises on Loch Ness are also available, as well as the Loch Ness Express ferry to Inverness. An interesting rural attraction lying close to the village is the Highland and Rare Breeds Croft, signposted from the bridge, open 10.00 to 18.00 except Saturday, March to October. There is an entrance charge (☎01320-366433).

GREAT GLEN WAY RANGERS

The Great Glen Way Rangers, who maintain the route you are following, have an office in the forest at Auchterawe, not far from Fort Augustus. They welcome feedback from walkers and are keen to hear about problems experienced along the route so that they can address them. Contact: Great Glen Way Rangers, Auchterawe, Fort Augustus, PH32 4BT; ☎01320-366633.

DAY 4

Fort Augustus to North Laggan

Start	Fort Augustus Swing Bridge – grid ref 379092
Finish	North Laggan – grid ref 300982
Distance	14km (9 miles)
Total Ascent	40m (130ft)
Maps	OS Landranger 34, OS Explorer 400, Harvey Great Glen Way
Terrain	A clear and firm canal-side track leads to Aberchalder. Tracks and paths beside Loch Oich can be wet and muddy.
Refreshments	There are plenty of restaurants, cafés, take-aways and bars around Fort Augustus. A couple of tearooms lie off-route at Aberchalder. A restaurant and bar is located at the Great Glen Water Park.
Public Transport	Regular daily Scottish Citylink buses link Fort Augustus and Laggan with Inverness and Fort William. The Loch Ness Express ferry links Fort Augustus with Dochgarroch, near Inverness.

This is a splendid day's walk, where the walls of the Great Glen rise closer to hand and there are often views of the high mountains further beyond. The Great Glen Way climbs up a steep flight of five locks as it follows the Caledonian Canal away from Fort Augustus. A lovely stretch of the canal gradually rises to Aberchalder, where it is worth making a slight detour to admire the Bridge of Oich. The summit level of the canal is at Loch Oich, which is passed using a stretch of General Wade's military road, as well as part of an old railway line. Richly wooded slopes are protected as a nature reserve on the way to North Laggan, where facilities are very limited.

Leave **Fort Augustus** by climbing from the swing bridge, alongside a fine flight of locks leading up from Loch Ness. Use the path on the same side as the **Caledonian Canal Visitor Centre.**

For map, see pp. 53–62.

The Caledonian Canal Visitor Centre stands beside the canal locks and is full of interesting heritage information.

CALEDONIAN CANAL VISITOR CENTRE

As walkers ascend the flight of five locks through Fort Augustus, metal disks along the way pose all sorts of questions about the Caledonian Canal, its history, construction and use. Visitors who want to find the answers are directed to the Caledonian Canal Visitor Centre, just across the road. A small exhibition space can be explored, there are books on sale about the canal, while British Waterways Scotland staff are on hand to deal with any queries. The centre is open 09.30 to 17.30, April to October, and entry is free (☎01320-366493).

After passing the top lock, the canal gradually bends to the left and views of Fort Augustus are lost. A covered overspill weir allows excess water to fall into the **River Oich,** and there are glimpses of the river from time to time, as both the canal and river run parallel. The canal passes a **power line** and bends gradually to the right. A fine row of pine trees grows along the opposite bank. Hazel trees are abundant along the bank being followed, though the woodland cover alongside the track is quite mixed. Tall pines flank the canal on both sides at **Kytra Lock.**

After passing Kytra Lock an **overspill weir** has to be crossed, and this could mean wet feet if there is excess water in the canal, though this would be a very rare occurrence. The canal broadens considerably where **Kytra Loch** was incorporated into its course. A variety of trees later flank the canal, but there are several particularly tall and graceful birch trees. When **Cullochy Lock** is reached, cross over the lock gates to pick up and follow a **track** on the other side of the canal. Look across the water to spot a large **overspill weir** to the River Oich. A clear track runs beside the canal and passes a **cottage** to reach the **Aberchalder Swing Bridge** and the busy A82 road.

A flight of five canal locks cuts the village of Fort Augustus in two, and proves immensely popular with visitors.

BRIDGE OF OICH

It is worth leaving the Great Glen Way for a few minutes and crossing the Aberchalder Swing Bridge to reach the Bridge of Oich. An older bridge was swept away in devastating floods during 1849, when the embankment of the Caledonian Canal was also breached. Five years elapsed before a new bridge was built, by a brewer-turned-engineer called James Dredge, from Bath. The Bridge of Oich looks like a slender suspension bridge, but was actually patented as a 'double cantilever', built on the 'taper principle'. The supporting chains gradually diminish as they spread outwards from the stout granite pillars that support them, and hold very little weight in the middle of the bridge. Apparently, if the bridge was ever severed in the middle, it would remain standing. The Bridge of Oich carried traffic up to 1932, but the busy A82 road now crosses a more solid-looking stone bridge nearby.

Follow a path alongside the canal, then cross a ladder stile on the left to continue along the shore of **Loch Oich.** Go through a kissing gate and turn right to cross an old railway bridge over the **Calder Burn.** The Great Glen Way reaches a couple of gates on the **Aberchalder Estate Road,** where a sign lists a number of facilities that may be of interest to walkers. These include a couple of bed and breakfast places, and a couple of cafés. These are all within easy reach of **Aberchalder Lodge.**

LOCH OICH

This is the smallest of the three lochs linked by the Caledonian Canal (not counting the much smaller Kytra Loch). It measures 6.5km (4 miles) in length and is only 0.5km (0.3 miles) across at its widest point. Loch Oich's greatest depth is 40.5m (133ft), but it had to be deepened at both ends to accommodate traffic using the Caledonian Canal. The surface level of the loch is 32m (105ft), which is also the summit level for the canal.

Turn right, away from the gates, to cross a bridge at a small waterfall. As the track, which is an old military road, runs gently uphill, watch out for a miniature **iron aqueduct** on the right, carrying water across the old railway line. Walk steeply down through a rocky, mossy cutting, crossing over an old railway tunnel, where both the track and old railway line have to avoid a **cliff** dropping sheer into the lake. The track briefly touches the lake shore and continues through woods, then runs through a meadow and passes an old **cottage.** Watch out for a crenelated **concrete arch** on the left, which supports the old railway trackbed. The track proceeds along the shore of Loch Oich, and there are views across it from time to time when the trees thin out. The ruins of **Invergarry Castle** might be seen on the far shore. Go through a gate and climb uphill a short way to continue along the old **railway trackbed.** The surroundings are vividly green and are managed as a nature reserve.

LEITERFEARN FOREST NATURE RESERVE

Leiterfearn features a lush, damp, vibrantly green woodland that is a mixture of ash, birch, elm and hazel. The steep slopes support cushions of moss and delicate ferns, as well as flowers in spring and fungi in autumn. It has the appearance of a jungle, yet it has been cut back twice to accommodate a road and railway. General Wade pushed a road through the woods around 1725, while the Invergarry and Fort Augustus Railway Company pushed a railway through, which opened in 1903. Both routes fell from favour, the road switching to the other side of the loch and the railway being abandoned in 1946.

The old **trackbed** features some cuttings where the ground can be wet and muddy, and there are later clumps of rhododendron before the route drifts to the right and lands on a narrow tarmac road at the **Great Glen Water Park.** A right turn off-route leads in a few paces to a bar and restaurant surrounded by wooden

A 'trimaran' passes the Great Glen Water Park on its way from Loch Oich to the Caledonian Canal at North Laggan.

Some walkers may need to detour to Invergarry in search of accommodation. The quickest and safest way to do this is to catch a bus.

chalets on the shores of **Loch Oich.** If a visit isn't required, then simply turn left and follow the quiet road to a junction with the busy **A82 road.** Cross the road with care at **North Laggan,** where facilities are particularly sparse. A sign points left, off-route along the main road, across the Laggan Swing Bridge, for the Well of the Seven Heads Store, if food, drink or an ATM are required. ◄

LAGGAN

Laggan (*Gaelic* – Lagan) is a sprawling settlement with no clear centre. North Laggan is close to the Laggan Swing Bridge, while South Laggan is the area near Laggan Locks, over 2 kilometres (1.25 miles) away. Facilities are limited to the Loch Lochy Youth Hostel, a couple of bed and breakfast places, a converted Dutch barge called 'Eagle', but known as 'The Inn on the Water', and a bar restaurant at the

Great Glen Water Park. Regular daily Scottish Citylink buses link Laggan with Inverness, Fort Augustus and Fort William.

WELL OF THE SEVEN HEADS

Some say it was a deliberate act, while others say it was an accident, but all agree that on 25th September 1663, Alexander MacDonald, Chief of Keppoch, and his brother Ranald, were killed by seven others during a clan dispute. While most of their kinsfolk seemed content to let the matter rest, Iain Lom, the Keppoch Bard, called for revenge, enlisting the support of MacDonald of Glengarry and Sir James MacDonald of Sleat. After two years, the seven culprits were tracked down to Inverlair, where they were slain and beheaded. The severed heads were washed in a well beside Loch Oich, then displayed at Invergarry Castle before being taken to Gallows Hill in Edinburgh on 7th December 1665. The Well of the Seven Heads is now enclosed in stone and bears a monument. The monument is crowned with seven unhappy-looking heads, surmounted by a hand holding a dagger. The tale of murder and revenge is carved around all four sides in English, Gaelic, French and Latin.

INVERGARRY

The village of Invergarry is on the 'wrong' side of Loch Oich to the Great Glen Way, but some walkers may need to go there if they cannot secure lodgings around Laggan. A small range of lodgings ranges from hostel to hotel accommodation. Regular daily Scottish Citylink buses link Invergarry with Inverness and Fort William. The Glengarry Visitor Centre, open from Easter to September, 10.30 to 16.30, has a small entrance charge and also operates as a Tourist Information Centre (☎01809-501424).

DAY 5

North Laggan to Gairlochy

Start	North Laggan – grid ref 300982
Finish	Gairlochy Bottom Lock – grid ref 176842
Distance	22km (13.5 miles)
Total Ascent	300m (985ft)
Maps	OS Landranger 34, OS Explorer 400, Harvey Great Glen Way
Terrain	Canal-side path, minor roads, forest tracks and clear, firm paths.
Refreshments	The Inn on the Water at Laggan Locks. Telford Tearoom at Gairlochy.
Public Transport	Regular daily Scottish Citylink buses link Laggan with Inverness, Fort Augustus and Fort William. There are schooldays-only bus services linking Gairlochy, Spean Bridge and Fort William, which will divert to Achnacarry on request to the driver.

This day starts with an easy walk through Laggan alongside the Caledonian Canal, but most of the day is spent on the northern shore of Loch Lochy, on forest tracks running parallel to the shore, and there is no exit from these until Clunes is reached. The slopes are often well wooded or forested, and timber harvesting and replanting ensures that over time, different places will feature different views. Detours from the Great Glen Way can be considered around Achnacarry, either to see St Ciaran's Church, tucked away in the woods, or to visit the Clan Cameron Museum. This is essentially Cameron country, or at least, it became Cameron country after the Camerons concluded a 350-year feud against the MacIntoshes! Bear in mind that Gairlochy has few facilities, and its bus service generally operates only on schooldays. If staying off-route, ask in advance if your accommodation provider can collect you.

For map, see pp. 42–52 Leave **North Laggan** by following a gravel path between the busy **A82 road** and the **Caledonian Canal**. Bracken gives way to broom, gorse and brambles. There is a view along the canal from high above a **mooring stage.** The path leads across a footbridge over a canal feeder, the **Allt an Lagain.** All of a sudden, there is access on the left to the **A82 road,** where a sign points along the road for **Loch Lochy Youth Hostel.** Take care if following the road as it can be very busy.

The path keeps off the road, and the woods alongside the canal are quite mixed, with broom and rhododendron scrub also noticed at first. Later, there is a slope of conifers alongside the canal, then the narrow path broadens to become a **grassy track** running along the top of an embankment. Pass the **Eagle,** which is a Dutch barge converted into a pub-restaurant-in-a-boat known as the 'Inn on the Water'. Keep to the left of a canal-side cottage to reach the double lock at **Laggan Locks.**

BATTLE OF THE SHIRTS

The seeds of this conflict were sown, as was often the case among Highland clans, with a perceived insult. Ranald Galda, of Clanranald, had been reared among the Frasers, and when he returned to his home a feast was prepared by way of welcome. As seven oxen were slaughtered, Ranald remarked that a few hens would have been sufficient, thus spurning the hospitality of his hosts. They called him 'Ranald of the Hens' and said that he could return to the Frasers if he didn't like it.

It was an uncomfortably hot day in 1544 when 300 Frasers faced a combined force of 600 MacDonalds and Camerons to settle the score at Laggan. Both sides had to put aside their hot and heavy woollen plaids and fight each other wearing long undershirts; hence the name 'Battle of the Shirts'. Neither side scored a victory, since the carnage was so great that only four Frasers and eight of their opponents were left standing at the conclusion of the battle.

View across Ceann Loch, which is part of Loch Lochy, towards the rugged slopes of Meall na Teanga.

Turn right to cross the lock gates over the canal at **Laggan Locks.** Walk between cottages to pick up and follow a causeway road, crossing boggy ground beside **Ceann Loch.** Pass some wooden lodges, then when a road junction is reached, turn left to follow another road until it crosses a bridge near **Kilfinnan Farm.** Turn right to follow a clear track uphill from the farm, enjoying views over the head of Loch Lochy. The gradient eases and the track keeps to the right as it passes the access for the **Highland Lodges.**

Go through a **tall gate** and continue straight ahead, reaching a junction of tracks near a **communication mast,** where a left turn is made down a forest track. The track is almost exclusively flanked by birch, which effectively screens views of conifers alongside. The track continues close to the shore of **Loch Lochy** and the trees are remarkably mixed, with conifers, alder and birch.

LOCH LOCHY

The level of Loch Lochy was raised 3.65m (12ft) during the construction of the Caledonian Canal. Its surface level is now 28.5m (94ft) above sea level, and its maximum depth is 40.5m (133ft). The loch is just short of 16km (10 miles) in length and only once exceeds 1.5km (1 mile) in width. It is said to be inhabited by a monster known as 'Lizzie', no doubt related to 'Nessie'.

Climb steeply uphill a short way from the shore and cross a bridge over the **Allt Glas-Dhoire**, walking among tall trees without any views, and pass a tall **gateway.** The track runs through younger forest where there is a margin of alder scrub, then runs through another area of mature forest before crossing a bridge over the **Allt Glas-Dhoire Mór.** On the next gentle ascent and descent, clear-felling allows good views across the loch, but these are lost as the track climbs through a more mature part of the forest, passing another **gateway** before descending gently. The track rises uphill, then later passes a gateway and small waterfall on the **Allt na Molaich.** The track undulates and passes commercial conifers, as well as self-seeded alder and birch scrub, along with bracken, brambles and tufts of heather.

The track runs parallel to the shore of Loch Lochy until it swings right and goes through a tall gate to reach a **car park.** Continue past a couple of houses and a couple of wooden cabins, one of which is the **Clunes Forest School.** ▶

Turn left along the B8005 road at **Clunes,** passing modest forestry houses and a large white house. Continue along the road as the land near Loch Lochy is very wet and boggy, supporting profuse growths of bog myrtle. A fine variety of trees grace the shores of Loch Lochy, so that the area is rather like an arboretum. The most striking conifers are the giant redwoods, or sequoias, while the most striking deciduous trees are the copper beeches. Continue along the road, crossing a bridge over the River Arkaig at **Bunarkaig,** where you reach a cluster of houses. ▶ Just up the road, another sign at a gateway invites visitors to make a detour to the **Clan Cameron Museum.**

Occasionally, the Great Glen Way Rangers station themselves at the Forest School and welcome the opportunity to have a chat with walkers.

A short detour could be made to St Ciaran's Church, built in a quiet woodland setting. Watch out for a sign showing the way along a track.

A detail from one of the stained glass windows in St Ciaran's Church, just off-route near Achnacarry.

CLAN CAMERON

The Clan Cameron has a long association with the Great Glen. Originally, there were three families – the McMartins of Letterfinlay, the McGillonies of Strone and the McSorlies of Glen Nevis. The first Chief of the combined families was Donald Dubh, born around 1400, and the most recent is Donald Angus Cameron of Locheil, the 27th Chief. Never shy of battle, the Camerons were described as 'fiercer than fierceness itself'. Their rallying cry was 'Sons of the hounds, come hither and get flesh!' The Camerons moved from Tor Castle to Achnacarry around 1660, and visitors will appreciate the attractions of the location, an easily defended mountain fastness with sheltered pasture.

The 19th Chief, the 'Gentle Locheil' supported Bonnie Prince Charlie in 1745, and in giving support, ensured that many other clans rallied to the cause. Despite early military success, the Prince's forces were soundly beaten at Culloden and Charles was lucky to escape with his life. In retribution for Locheil's support, the Duke of Cumberland destroyed the original timber-built Achnacarry House in 1746, and Locheil fled into exile. The current stone-built Achnacarry House dates from 1802, and the Clan Cameron has distinguished itself by raising generations of soldiery for the Queen's Own Cameron Highlanders. Achnacarry House was occupied by the military for most of the Second World War, when it was the Commando Basic Training Centre, featuring one of the most gruelling military training regimes in the world.

CLAN CAMERON MUSEUM

If you are a Cameron – and that includes members of nearly seventy 'sept' or sub-branch families! – then you should feel obliged to make a detour to the Clan Cameron Museum at Achnacarry. The Museum, housed in a whitewashed 17th-century croft, is open each afternoon from Easter to mid-October, 13.30 to 17.00, but in July and August it is open from 11.00 to 17.00. There should be a notice by the gates on the B8005 road if the museum is open. There is an entrance charge (☎01397-712090, website **www.clan-cameron.org**).

Follow the **B8005 road** onwards, until a left turn is waymarked down a clear gravel path, gradually descending across a slope of gnarled oaks, slender birch, beech and alder. The path wanders along the shore of Loch Lochy and crosses **two footbridges** as it runs round a small bay. Later, the path drifts away from the shore to cross a footbridge over the **Allt Coire Choille-rais.** Densely packed conifers allow little light to reach the ground, but birch trees fringe the loch shore. Later, the path passes fine beech trees, where bright green moss thrives, covering boulders and fallen tree trunks. Cross a **footbridge** and follow the path onwards, and look out for a prominent little lighthouse and signs that indicate where the Caledonian Canal leaves the loch. The path climbs steeply from the shore and reaches the **B8005 road** again.

Cross the road and follow the path as it undulates across a forested slope, just above the road. The path joins the road just before a **junction,** where forking left leads down to a swing bridge over the Caledonian Canal at **Gairlochy Bottom Lock.**

GAIRLOCHY

Take note of the number of times Gairlochy has won, or come runner-up in, the 'Waterway Length Competition'. Also take note that facilities in the area are few. Gairlochy is hardly a village, but merely a scattering of houses. The Telford Tearoom stands near the canal, while a mere handful of bed and breakfast places lie along the road nearby. The Gairlochy Holiday Park offers a campsite in the direction of Spean Bridge, and there is a budget bunkhouse. Any further services are located around Spean Bridge.

SPEAN BRIDGE

Spean Bridge is 6 kilometres (4 miles) away from Gairlochy. Most of the distance is along and up the quiet B8004 road, passing Mucomir Power Station and the Gairlochy Holiday Park, as well as a couple of bed and breakfast places. The Station House reminds passers-by that a railway once ran through this part of the Great Glen. The road eventually reaches the celebrated Commando Memorial, dating

from 1952, on the main A82 road, from where a descent leads to Spean Bridge and its services. A bridge built by General Wade in 1736 was the first to span the rocky gorge beside the village.

There are a few accommodation options around Spean Bridge, including a hotel. There is a post office shop, with an ATM outside, as well as a take-away. There are regular daily Scottish Citylink bus services to and from Fort William, Fort Augustus and Inverness, as well as Rapson's Highland Country buses running to and from Fort William. Bear in mind that there is a schooldays-only bus linking Fort William and Gairlochy with Spean Bridge, but most accommodation providers will provide lifts to and from Gairlochy if given due notice. There are trains from Spean Bridge to Fort William and Glasgow. The Kingdom of Scotland Visitor Centre at Spean Bridge also serves as the Tourist Information Centre (☎01397-712999).

The Commando Memorial occupies a splendid site, with rugged mountains leading the eye to Ben Nevis.

DAY 6

Gairlochy to Fort William

Start	Gairlochy Bottom Lock – grid ref 176842
Finish	Railway Station, Fort William – grid ref 105742
Distance	17km (10.5 miles)
Total Ascent	10m (35ft)
Maps	OS Landranger 41, OS Explorers 392 & 400, Harvey Great Glen Way
Terrain	A long, clear canal-side track, followed by low-level paths, tracks and roads near the coast.
Refreshments	Tearoom at Gairlochy. Bar and restaurant at Banavie. Shops and bars at Corpach. Shops and take-aways at Caol. Plenty of bars, restaurants and cafés around Fort William.
Public Transport	There is a schooldays-only bus service linking Fort William, Gairlochy and Spean Bridge. Rapson's Highland Country buses link Banavie, Corpach and Caol with Fort William, as well as running all the town services around Fort William. There are also trains between Fort William, Banavie and Corpach, as well as to Spean Bridge and Glasgow.

Most of this final day's walk is actually on a long and narrow 'island', flanked on one side by the Caledonian Canal and on the other side by the River Lochy. This is an easy day's walk, descending in stages while following a clear canal-side track past locks. A series of roads, tracks and paths run close to the coast on the way to Fort William. Facilities increase as the route progresses, and Fort William offers the largest concentration of lodgings and other services encountered since the start of the Great Glen Way in Inverness.

For map, see pp. 29–41.

Leave **Gairlochy** and its swing bridge by following a track past **Gairlochy Bottom Lock.** The track drops a little, then crosses an **overspill weir** and enjoys a fine view of the broad and shingly **River Lochy.** Looking ahead you can see Ben Nevis rising majestically from the

A boat sails along the Caledonian Canal between Gairlochy Top Lock and Gairlochy Bottom Lock.

further reaches of the Great Glen. Tall beech trees grace the canal-side, and later, on the far bank of the canal, a knoll bearing distinctive pine trees is an old **burial ground.** Also look across the canal to spot an inflowing stream, then reach the attractive **Moy Swing Bridge.**

MOY SWING BRIDGE

The Moy Swing Bridge simply allows the farmer from Moy to drive tractors and trailers down to his river-side meadows. Canal traffic, meanwhile, relies on a keeper to open and close the bridge on demand. However, the bridge is not mechanised, and only one half can be opened manually at a time; hence the need for a small boat so that the keeper can row across and open the other half.

Continue along the track, passing gorse bushes for a while, which allow views across small meadows near the **River Lochy.** These views are closed off later as trees flank the canal-side. Further along, the canal crosses the **Loy Aqueduct** over the River Loy.

LOY AQUEDUCT

To see the Loy Aqueduct properly, you must turn sharp left, well after crossing over the aqueduct, to follow a track down to it, then retrace your steps afterwards. It is a splendid structure, with the River Loy flowing through a large central arch, while smaller arches on either side allow passage for man and beast.

The track later crosses an **overspill,** where excess water flows down into the River Lochy. Look across the canal to see a knoll crowned with a few pine trees, which is another old **burial ground.** The track rises gently, then falls gently, passing abundant birch trees on the little hill of **Druim na h-Atha,** followed by a **cottage.** Continue enjoying the variety of trees alongside, and look across the water to spot a stream feeding water into the canal.

It is quite possible to cross the **Sheangain Aqueduct** without noticing, but try and include a few minutes to have a look at it.

SHEANGAIN AQUEDUCT

Use a narrow path to descend from the embankment, then there is a view of three arched tunnels, two arches carrying water from the Allt Sheangain and another arch covering a stone-paved passage for man and his animals.

TOR CASTLE

Not far from the Sheangain Aqueduct, Tor Castle overlooks the River Lochy. It was built by the MacIntoshes, who vacated it towards the end of the 13th century. Some time later it was occupied by the Camerons, sparking a feud between the two clans that spanned some 350 years, continuing even after the Camerons abandoned the property in 1660 and went to settle in Achnacarry.

The canal curves gently left and right and for brief periods there are no signs of habitation, while a splendid variety of trees flank both banks. Follow the track

The lock at the top of Neptune's Staircase is the first of eight locks falling in quick succession at Banavie.

onwards, passing through a **gate** beside tall pines. **Banavie Top Jetty** is reached, where there are toilets for canal users. Walk downhill in stages alongside the celebrated stepped locks known as **Neptune's Staircase** to reach the busy A830 at **Banavie Swing Bridge.**

NEPTUNE'S STAIRCASE

Neptune's Staircase is an inspired name for the tightly packed series of eight canal locks at Banavie. The arrangement is difficult to see in its entirety, and the best views are those seen in the aerial shots used for postcards. Canal cruisers can pass from top to bottom in about 90 minutes, including passage through the road and rail swing bridges at the bottom, but the time taken can almost double if craft pass through in the other direction at the same time.

BANAVIE

Banavie (*Gaelic* – Banbhaidh) is a little village with only a few facilities. The Moorings Hotel and a couple of guest houses are available, along with a canal-side gift shop that also offers teas. There are regular daily bus and train services to and from Corpach and Fort William, as well as a schooldays-only service back to Gairlochy.

Cross the busy A830 road with care and turn left to pass **Banavie Station.** Turn right at a junction, to walk over a level crossing, and continue along the road almost as far as a little pub called **Lochy.** Head right, as directed up a path, to reach the track beside the Caledonian Canal again. Continue straight along the broad gravel track, flanked on the right by grassy, flowery waterside banks, with tall beech trees on the left often obscuring views of **Caol.** The canal describes a broad and graceful curve to the right, later passing an **overspill,** where excess water from the canal flows down into Loch Linnhe. When the **Corpach Double Lock** is reached, the Great Glen Way turns left down a path, but walkers might wish to continue to the nearby terminus of the Caledonian Canal at the Corpach Basin and explore the village of **Corpach** too.

CORPACH

Corpach (*Gaelic* – A' Chorpaich) is an interesting little village, well worth a visit, overlooking the western sea terminus of the Caledonian Canal. There is public access to the Corpach Sea Lock and Corpach Basin, where boats may be moored while they wait for a favourable tide. The Narrows nearby are dominated by a huge pulp and paper mill, which chews up trees from the surrounding forests. A popular attraction in the village is 'Treasures of the Earth', which focuses on mines, minerals, gemstones and fossils, for those with an interest in geology. Open throughout the year, except Christmas and January, 09.30 to 19.00 in summer and 10.00 to 17.00 in winter (☎01397-772283). There is an entrance charge.

Corpach has a budget bunkhouse and independent hostel, as well as a few bed and breakfast places and a hotel. There is a post office inside the Co-op store, and an ATM outside. Toilets are available in the Kilmallie Hall, when open, while canal users have access to toilets near the canal office.

Another shop and a bar are also available, and there are regular daily bus and train services to and from neighbouring Banavie and Fort William.

Step down from the stout embankment of the **Caledonian Canal,** following a path across a **footbridge** below the overspill weir. Walk along a gravel coastal path hemmed in between the shore of Loch Linnhe and a **sports pitch,** to reach **Erracht Drive,** which is flanked by a broad coastal green, in the village of **Caol.**

CAOL

Caol (*Gaelic* – Caol Loch Abar) is a village close to The Narrows, where Loch Linnhe turns a right-angle corner and becomes known as Loch Eil. There are a small number of bed and breakfast establishments, a post office, toilets, a couple of shops and take-aways, as well as regular daily bus services to and from neighbouring Fort William, Corpach and Banavie.

Continue along **Erracht Drive,** turning left at the end along **Glenmallie Road.** Turn right at a bus stop to follow the B8006 road, Kilwallie Road, passing a couple of bed and breakfast places and a primary school on the way out of the village. The road runs parallel to the **River Lochy,** and when it rises onto a railway bridge, turn right to cross the **Soldier's Bridge.** This is a long wooden footbridge mounted on top of a pipe, running parallel to the railway bridge over the river. Stepping down from the bridge, consider making a detour beneath the railway line to visit the nearby **Inverlochy Castle.**

INVERLOCHY CASTLE

The Comyns were a powerful Scottish family with two branches, the Red Comyns and the Black Comyns. The Red Comyns built Inverlochy Castle (*Gaelic* – Inbhir Lòchaidh) in 1280 and surrounded it with a moat connected to the River Lochy. The four-square thick stone walls are protected by drum towers at each corner, and the largest tower is Comyn's Tower. There was probably a timber-built Great Hall inside the walls. The castle is always open and there is no entrance charge.

The Red Comyns and Black Comyns supported John Balliol's claim to the Scottish throne, and therefore attracted the enmity of Robert the Bruce. The MacDonalds supported Bruce, and in 1297 their vessels engaged Comyn vessels off Inverlochy, resulting in the sinking of two ships. The Comyns were later defeated in battle at Inverurie in May 1308, and Bruce granted Inverlochy Castle to the MacDonalds.

In the 15th century the MacDonalds were often in conflict with the Stuarts, who sat on the Scottish throne. Following a MacDonald raid on Inverness, James I sent a force commanded by the Earl or Mar to Inverlochy in 1431. As the army camped by the river they were picked off by MacDonald bowmen from the strategic hill of Tom na Faire, losing a thousand men. In 1645 there was another battle, this time between the Royalist army of Charles I, led by the Marquis of Montrose, with MacDonald support, and a Covenanting force led by the Marquis of Argyll with Campbell support. Again, the strategic hill of Tom na Faire was put to good use by the Royalists, and despite their smaller force, they suffered only 20 casualties, while their opponents suffered 1500.

Following the construction of a wooden fort at Fort William in 1654, which was in turn replaced by a stone fort in 1690, Inverlochy Castle fell from favour. Military might was further consolidated when General Wade built a road from Fort William to Fort Augustus, passing Inverlochy Castle and completed in 1727. The castle was abandoned and was used by the Invergarry Ironworks from 1729 to 1736 as a store for pig iron.

Cross a **bridge** over the **tailrace** stream flowing from the Alcan aluminium works. Turn right to pick up and follow a path into a field, drifting left away from a narrow footbridge over the tailrace. The powerful flow hits the little footbridge so hard that the water rises up and the structure vibrates! Follow the riverside path past a **sports pitch,** then go through a **kissing gate** and continue across a rushy meadow. Enter a woodland and follow the path across a couple of small **footbridges.** Alder trees tend to screen the river from sight, and also screen the **Inverlochy** suburbs of Fort William. Turn left, then right to cross a bridge over the **River Nevis.** Ben Nevis rises far inland to the left, while the waters of Loch Linnhe are nearby.

Briefly follow a brick-paved road past a few houses, then follow a clear path alongside a shinty pitch. (Shinty is a popular Gaelic sport that resembles hockey.) The path reaches a busy roundabout beside **McDonald's** restaurant in **Fort William.** Keep right to walk round the roundabout and reach the ruins of the **Old Fort,** where a few low walls stand above the shore of Loch Linnhe. A **stone monument** marks the end of the Great Glen Way.

THE OLD FORT

The first fort on this site was a timber structure, built by General Monck to house 250 men. He referred to it as 'the fort of Inverlochy' in 1654, when writing to advise Oliver Cromwell of its completion. A stone fort was constructed in 1690 by General Mackay, housing 1000 men and defended by fifteen guns. It was named in honour of King William, a member of the Dutch House of Orange, who fought a decisive battle against King James in that year. William ruled Britain jointly with his wife, Mary, James's daughter. General Gordon attacked the fort during the 1715 rebellion, then in 1746 Sir Ewen Cameron attacked it. The fort was largely dismantled and the land bought by the West Highland Railway Company in 1889. They pushed a railway through the site, leaving only

Even in the middle of May, there could be a considerable depth of snow and ice on top of Ben Nevis.

the small portion of the original walls seen today, which includes a sally port. The original stone-arched gateway to the fort was rebuilt and now serves as the entrance to a small graveyard off the busy Belford Road in Fort William.

To walk from the **Old Fort** into town, the best way is to double back to **McDonald's** restaurant, then cross a road and walk across Morrison's supermarket car park to reach the railway station or bus station. There is immediate access to the centre of **Fort William** by way of an underpass. (See the introduction to the South to North route for a description of Fort William.)

APPENDIX 1

ROUTE SUMMARY

GREAT GLEN WAY, SOUTH TO NORTH

Day	Leg	Distance		Ascent	
		km	miles	m	ft
1	Fort William to Gairlochy	17	10.5	40	130
2	Gairlochy to North Laggan	22	13.5	330	1080
3	North Laggan to Fort Augustus	14	9	30	100
4	Fort Augustus to Invermoriston	13	8	300	985
5	Invermoriston to Drumnadrochit	23	14	600	1970
6	Drumnadrochit to Inverness	29	18	500	1640

GREAT GLEN WAY, NORTH TO SOUTH

Day	Leg	Distance		Ascent	
		km	miles	m	ft
1	Inverness to Drumnadrochit	29	18	540	1770
2	Drumnadrochit to Invermoriston	23	14	590	1935
3	Invermoriston to Fort Augustus	13	8	320	1050
4	Fort Augustus to North Laggan	14	9	40	130
5	North Laggan to Gairlochy	22	13.5	300	985
6	Gairlochy to Fort William	17	10.5	10	35

APPENDIX 2

TIMELINE HISTORY

The following timeline history is biased in favour of events that took place in the Great Glen and the Highlands of Scotland, at the expense of events that took place around Edinburgh or the Scots/English border.

7500BC – Mesolithic hunter-gatherers made their way along the Highland coast, carrying simple stone tools and pots. They left little trace of their passing, except where they settled long enough to create 'middens', or rubbish dumps of bones and shell fragments.

3000BC – Neolithic migration through Scotland, with the construction of chambered cairns. The 'Fortingall Yew' sprouted around this time and probably remains the oldest living tree in Europe.

300BC – During the Iron Age, Celtic tribes from southern Scotland and Ireland migrated northwards, building forts, or duns, and stone towers, or brochs.

AD43 – Emissaries were sent from the Orkney Islands to make contact with Claudius during the Roman conquest of Britain. A tribe living in the Great Glen was named the Caledones at this time; a name which was later used to describe almost all the tribes living in the Highlands of Scotland.

AD84 – The battle of Mons Graupius, thought to be in the Grampian, or Moray region. Agricola led four legions of Roman soldiers into battle against the native Caledonii, who were led by Calgacus. Although the Romans won the battle, they were never able to subdue the Highlands, and withdrew southwards. The Romans were impressed by the hardy nature of the tribes, while Tacitus said they had red hair and large limbs.

AD122 – Hadrian's Wall was constructed across northern England.

AD142 – The Antonine Wall was constructed across central Scotland.

AD250 – The 'Scots', who were an Irish tribe, began to conduct raids along the western seaboard of Scotland.

AD297 – A Roman writer, Eumenius, was the first to mention the Picts by name, although it is thought they were already well established in the land.

AD367 – The Scots, Saxons and Franks came into greater contact with the Picts as they worked their way into Scotland.

AD392 – St Ninian introduces Christianity to the far south of Scotland at Whithorn.

AD400–500 – The legendary Pictish warrior Cruithne was said to have ruled over much of Scotland for 100 years. On his death, each of his seven sons ruled over part of his kingdom. Around AD500, the Western Highlands were already under Scots control, while Fergus established the kingdom of Dalriada, based around Argyll and the islands. The Picts found themselves pushed more to the north and east of Scotland.

AD563 – St Columba was exiled from Ireland and settled on Iona.

AD565 – St Columba travelled through the Great Glen and is credited with seeing the Loch Ness 'monster' on his way to Inverness. He met the Pictish king Brude and duelled with his magician Briochan. Around this time, there were essentially four distinct civilisations in Scotland: the northern Picts and southern kinsmen, the Scots of Dalriada, the Britons in central Scotland, with the Saxons and Angles further south. This situation led to a period of conflict and strife. Cumin, a follower of Columba, established a monastic settlement in the middle of the Great Glen.

AD603 – King Aedan of Dalriada united the Scots and Picts in an attempt to drive the Angles southwards into Northumbria. He was defeated in battle.

AD657–685 – Bridei, a Pictish ruler, attacked the Argyll capital of the Scots and subdued them, and later launched an assault against the expanding Northumbrian kingdom, leading to a short period of Pictish domination in Scotland.

AD706–724 – The Pictish ruler Neachtan worried about religious authority and banished Christian monks from his kingdom. However, he later relented and joined a religious community.

AD731–761 – Oengus Mac Fergus became the first king of both the Picts and the Scots, though he was unable to take the kingdom of Strathclyde. After his death, the Scots dissociated themselves from Pictish rule.

AD780 – Invaders from Scandinavia appeared in small numbers.

AD789–820 – A series of rulers, some Pictish and some Scots, ensured that the two kingdoms were basically unified throughout this period.

AD839 – Increasing numbers of Norse invaders caused huge problems. The Picts and Scots united, but were defeated by the invaders, leaving the two kingdoms severed from each other.

AD842–848 – Kenneth Mac Alpin, king of the Scots at Dalriada, moved to Scone and took with him the Lia Fáil, or Stone of Destiny, now known as the Stone of

Scone. This ancient stone, reputedly carried by the Celts from Scythia to Ireland, and thence to Scotland, was always associated with the coronation of kings. With its aid, and much political and physical manoeuvring, Mac Alpin became the first true King of the Scots. The official language was Gaelic, as the Pictish language and culture quickly expired. However, Norse influence remained strong throughout the region.

AD850 – Kenneth Mac Alpin conducts a series of raids on Northumbria.

AD900 – Constantin II attempted to absorb Norse settlers into the emerging kingdom of Scotland.

1005–1034 – Malcolm II achieved Scottish unity and expelled the English.

1040 – Duncan, heir of Malcolm, was killed by Macbeth, but not in the manner described by Shakespeare.

1057 – Macbeth was killed by Malcolm III, who took the throne and instituted the royal House of Canmore.

1093 – Death of St Margaret, founder of the modern city of Edinburgh, and wife of Malcolm III.

1124–1153 – David I introduced Norman culture to Scotland and built several abbeys in southern Scotland, including Jedburgh, Kelso, Melrose and Dryburgh.

1156 – Somerled, progenitor of the great clans MacDonald and Ranald, led a force against the Norse and became ruler of old Dalriada, though the islands remained nominally under Norse control.

1263 – The Norse relinquished control over the Hebrides after the Battle of Largs.

1280 – Inverlochy Castle was built by the Comyns at the foot of Ben Nevis.

1290 – The Scots queen Margaret, also known as the 'Maid of Norway', died on her way to marry Edward, son of Edward I of England. The Scots asked Edward I to decide who should rule Scotland out of a total of 13 claimants. Edward chose John Balliol, a man he could easily control.

1297–1305 – William Wallace led a violent campaign against the English, and was eventually captured and executed.

1306–1329 – Robert the Bruce strove to gain the Scottish throne. During this campaign he was supported by the MacDonalds, and gave them Inverlochy Castle in 1308. After the defeat of Edward II at Bannockburn, the Treaty of Northampton recognised Scottish sovereignty.

1368 – Edinburgh Castle was built.

1371–1390 – Robert II founded the royal House of Stewart. The king was often in conflict with the barons, as well as occasionally at war with the English.

1400 – Birth of Donald Dubh, who became the first chief of the Clan Cameron, who were often in dispute with their Great Glen neighbours the MacIntoshes.

1431 – The MacDonalds had raided Inverness, so James I sent a force commanded by the Earl or Mar to Inverlochy. The MacDonalds defeated them in the First Battle of Inverlochy.

1472 – Orkney and Shetland passed from Norse to Scottish control.

1488–1515 – The Highlands received little interference during the reign of James IV, and the king was eventually killed in war against the English at Flodden.

1542 – James V was defeated in battle by Henry VIII at Solway Moss.

1544 – The Battle of the Shirts took place at Laggan in the Great Glen.

1560–1587 – A time of political and religious strife. Mary, Queen of Scots, travelled in 1560 from Catholic France to Calvinist Scotland and married Lord Darnley in 1565. He was murdered in 1567, and Mary married the Earl of Bothwell, resulting in her expulsion from Scotland. Imprisoned by her father's cousin Elizabeth I, Mary was executed in 1587.

1603 – As Elizabeth I died without an heir, Mary's son, James VI of Scotland, was also crowned James I of England, although the Scottish and English parliaments remained separate. Political and religious strife continued.

1638–1643 – Both the Scottish and English parliaments rebelled against the rule of Charles I. The authority of Charles had already been challenged by the National Covenant in Scotland, and this led to Presbyterianism becoming the leading faith in Scotland. England descended into Civil War.

1645 – During the Second Battle of Inverlochy, the Civil War gave long-standing rival clans a chance to settle differences. The Marquis of Montrose, with MacDonald support, fought on the Royalist side. A Covenanting force led by the Marquis of Argyll with Campbell support, fought on the Parliamentarian side. The Royalists won, but retribution was swift and terrible.

1649–1652 – Following the execution of Charles I, Oliver Cromwell was made Lord Protector. He initiated a bloody campaign to clear the Scottish Highlands of Royalist support.

1654 – A wooden fort was built by General Monck, and referred to as 'the fort of Inverlochy', following the abandonment of Inverlochy Castle nearby.

1660 – The Restoration of the Monarchy. Charles II was invited back to England and the Covenanters were persecuted throughout Scotland. The Camerons abandoned Tor Castle and moved to Achnacarry.

1663–1665 – The 'Keppoch' murders, and the fierce retribution that resulted in the beheading of seven murderers at Inverlair, commemorated at the Well of the Seven Heads in the Great Glen.

1688–1689 – James VII of Scotland (and II of England) was ousted from the throne in favour of his daughter Mary, and her husband William of Orange. James's supporters were known as 'Jacobites' and were defeated at the Battle of Killiecrankie. Presbyterianism was re-established in Scotland.

1690 – General Mackay replaced 'the fort of Inverlochy' with a stone fort, which he named Fort William, in honour of the new king.

1692 – Urquhart Castle was rendered unusable. Highlanders who refused to support the king were slaughtered at the infamous Massacre of Glencoe.

1707 – The Scottish and English parliaments were united during the reign of Queen Anne.

1714 – With the death of Queen Anne, George I, descended from a daughter of James VI of Scotland, was crowned king, inaugurating the Hanoverian succession.

1715 – The First Jacobite Rebellion, following which a fort was established in the middle of the Great Glen.

1725 – General Wade began constructing roads through the Highlands.

1726 – The first plans for the Caledonian Canal through the Great Glen were drawn, but nothing was achieved on the ground.

1736 – General Wade built the High Bridge over a gorge at Spean Bridge.

1745–1746 – The Second Jacobite Rebellion, led by 'Bonnie Prince Charlie', who was a grandson of James VII of Scotland. Following initial surprising victories, his army of Highlanders pushed as far south as Derby. Charles would have pressed on to London, but for the counsel of his advisers. However, once he turned back towards Scotland, the Duke of Cumberland pursued the Scots to bloody defeat at Culloden, and wreaked havoc through the Great Glen. Charles was lucky to be able to escape with his life, aided at the end by Flora MacDonald. The fort in the middle of the Great Glen was rebuilt and named Fort Augustus after the 'Butcher' Duke of Cumberland.

1788 – The death of 'Bonnie Prince Charlie' in Rome. (Interestingly, an early 19th-century monument raised in the Vatican in honour of the last of the Stuarts was partly funded by the Hanoverian King George IV.)

1790 – The Forth and Clyde Canal was opened through central Scotland.

1800 – The beginning of the brutal 'Highland Clearances' led to the massive depopulation of the Highlands, with much farmland turned over to sheep pasture. While some people moved elsewhere in Scotland, most were forced to emigrate to North America.

1803–1822 – The Caledonian Canal was cut through the Great Glen. Tourism in the area began to develop apace.

1837 – Coronation of Queen Victoria.

1842–1846 – Railways finally linked London with Glasgow and Edinburgh. Fort William was lit using oil lamps.

1848 – Queen Victoria purchased the Balmoral Estate in the Highlands.

1849 – The Potato Famine hit the Highlands particularly hard, leading to one final clearance of the poorest part of the population from the land.

1854 – The Bridge of Oich was constructed by James Dredge at Aberchalder.

1855 – The Inverness and Nairn Railway was opened.

1864 – The Creag Dunain Hospital opens near Inverness.

1876 – The site of Fort Augustus was given to the Benedictines, who built an abbey there.

1883 – A pony track was constructed from Glen Nevis to the summit of Ben Nevis.

1886 – Foundation of the Scottish Home Rule Association.

1889 – The West Highland Railway reaches Fort William.

1895 – The development of a hydroelectric plant leads to electric lighting for Fort William.

1901 – The death of Queen Victoria.

1903 – The Invergarry and Fort Augustus Railway was opened, but was never extended through the Great Glen to Inverness as originally planned.

1928 – The Foundation of the Scottish National Party.

1931 – The British Aluminium (later Alcan) plant opened near Fort William, powered by an extensive hydroelectric scheme.

1934 – First photograph of the Loch Ness 'monster' published, leading to an influx of visitors and the further development of the tourist trade.

1940–1945 – During the Second World War, Commandos were based at Achnacarry House, enduring one of the world's toughest training regimes.

1946 – The Inverness and Fort Augustus Railway was closed.

1952 – Queen Elizabeth, the Queen Mother, unveiled the Commando Memorial above Spean Bridge.

1953 – Coronation of Queen Elizabeth II.

1964 – The Forth Road Bridge was opened near Edinburgh. The Scottish Pulp and Paper Mill was opened near Fort William.

1970 – The North Sea oil industry was developed, leading to increased prosperity in some parts of the Highlands.

1973 – The United Kingdom joined the Common Market.

1979–2000 – Scotland voted in two referenda on the issue of devolution, involving many years of debate, resulting in the election of a Scottish parliament.

2000 – Inverness was granted a city charter.

2002 – The Great Glen Way was officially opened by Prince Andrew, Earl of Inverness.

2003 – The Land Reform (Scotland) Act came into force, clarifying and guaranteeing rights of access to the Scottish countryside.

APPENDIX 3

USEFUL INFORMATION

Great Glen Way
Great Glen Way Rangers, Auchterawe, Fort Augustus, Inverness-shire, PH32 4BT,
☎01320-366633, email greatglenway@highland.gov.uk
Great Glen Way official website, **www.greatglenway.com**
Scottish Outdoor Access Code, **www.outdooraccess-scotland.com**

Caledonian Canal
Caledonian Canal Office, Seaport Marina, Muirtown Wharf, Inverness, IV3 5LE,
☎01463-233140
Caledonian Canal Visitor Centre, Fort Augustus, ☎01320-366493

Public Transport
Contact Traveline Scotland, ☎0870-6082608, **www.travelinescotland.com**, for
up-to-date information about any trains, buses or ferries in Scotland
Inverness Airport, ☎01463-232471
Virgin Trains, **www.virgintrains.co.uk**
First ScotRail, **www.firstgroup.com/scotrail**
Eurolines, **www.eurolines.com**
National Express, **www.nationalexpress.co.uk**
Scottish Citylink, **www.citylink.co.uk**
Rapson's Highland Country Buses, **www.rapsons.com**
Loch Ness Express Ferry, **www.lochnessexpress.com**

Accommodation
The Great Glen Way Accommodation and Services Guide contains an up-to-date
list of accommodation options, as well as notes about a wealth of services along
the course of the Great Glen Way. The guide is available free from the Great Glen
Way Rangers or Tourist Information Centres in the area.

Visit Scotland, ☎0845-2255121 (from UK) or +44-1506-832121 (from abroad),
www.visitscotland.com (to make credit card bookings by telephone)

Scottish Youth Hostels Association, **www.syha.org.uk**

Tourist Information Centres
Fort William – TIC, Cameron Square, Fort William, PH33 6AJ,
☎01397-703781, email fortwilliam@host.co.uk

Spean Bridge – Kingdom of Scotland Visitor Centre, Spean Bridge, PH34 4EP,
☎01397-712999, email treasures@kingdomofscotland.co.uk

Glengarry Visitor Centre – Invergarry, PH35 4HJ,
☎01809-501424

Fort Augustus – TIC, Car Park, Fort Augustus, PH32 4DD,
☎01320-366367, email fortaugustus@host.co.uk

Drumnadrochit – TIC, The Village Car Park, Drumnadrochit, IV63 6TX,
☎01456-459050, email drumnadrochit@host.co.uk

Inverness – TIC, Castle Wynd, Inverness, IV2 3BJ,
☎01463-234353, email inverness@host.co.uk

Tourist Attractions
West Highland Museum, Fort William, ☎01397-702169
Treasures of the Earth, Corpach, ☎01397-772283
Clan Cameron Museum, Achnacarry, ☎01397-712090
Highland and Rare Breeds Croft, Fort Augustus, ☎01320-366433
Urquhart Castle, Drumnadrochit, ☎01456-450551
Original Loch Ness Monster Centre, Drumnadrochit, ☎01456-450432
Official Loch Ness 2000 Exhibition, Drumnadrochit, ☎01456-450573
Inverness Museum and Art Gallery, Inverness, ☎01463-234353

Emergency Services
For police, ambulance, fire, mountain rescue or coastguard, dial 999 or 112

APPENDIX 4

GAELIC–ENGLISH GLOSSARY

The oldest place names in the Great Glen are Gaelic, since the language of the Picts has been lost. Gaelic thrives in the Highlands, and road signs throughout the region are often bilingual. Gaelic place names appear in abundance on maps, and they are often highly descriptive of landscape features.

Gaelic	English	Gaelic	English
Abhainn	River	*Fionn*	Fair
Allt	Stream	*Gaoithe*	Wind
Ard	High	*Garbh*	Rough
Ath	Ford	*Gearr*	Sharp
Auch	Field	*Glais*	Stream
Bal/Bally	Township	*Glas/Ghlas*	Grey
Bàn/Bhàn	White	*Gleann*	Glen/Valley
Bealach	Pass/Col	*Guala*	Shoulder
Beag/Bheag	Small	*Inbhir*	Confluence
Ben/Beinn/Bheinn	Mountain	*Innis*	Island/Field
Breac/Bhreac	Speckled	*Iolaire*	Eagle
Biorach	Pointed	*Lagan*	Hollow
Buidhe	Yellow	*Leac*	Flat rock
Caisteal	Castle	*Leathan*	Broad
Caol	Narrow	*Loch*	Lake
Caorach	Rowanberry	*Lochan*	Small lake
Carn	Cairn	*Maol/Mhaoile*	Bald
Cioch/Ciche	Breast	*Meall*	Rounded hill
Cir/Chir	Comb/Crest	*Mhuileann*	Mill
Clachan	Farm/Hamlet	*Monadh*	Mountain
Cnoc	Small hill	*Mór/Mhór*	Big
Coire/Choire	Corrie	*Mullach*	Summit
Coille	Wood	*Odhar*	Dappled
Creag	Crag	*Oighe*	Youth
Dearg	Red	*Reamhar*	Fat
Donn	Brown	*Righ*	King
Dubh	Black	*Ruadh*	Russet
Dun	Fort	*Suidhe*	Seat
Eas	Waterfall	*Torr*	Small hill
Eilean	Island	*Uaine*	Green
Fada/Fhada	Long	*Uisge*	Water

LISTING OF CICERONE GUIDES

BACKPACKING
The End to End Trail
Three Peaks, Ten Tors
Backpacker's Britain Vol 1 – Northern England
Backpacker's Britain Vol 2 – Wales
Backpacker's Britain Vol 3 – Northern Scotland
The Book of the Bivvy
NORTHERN ENGLAND LONG-DISTANCE TRAILS
The Dales Way
The Reiver's Way
The Alternative Coast to Coast
A Northern Coast to Coast Walk
The Pennine Way
Hadrian's Wall Path
The Teesdale Way
FOR COLLECTORS OF SUMMITS
The Relative Hills of Britain
Mts England & Wales Vol 2 – England
Mts England & Wales Vol 1 – Wales
BRITISH CYCLE GUIDES
The Cumbria Cycle Way
Land's End to John O'Groats – Cycle Guide
Rural Rides No.1 – West Surrey
Rural Rides No.2 – East Surrey
South Lakeland Cycle Rides
Border Country Cycle Routes
Lancashire Cycle Way
CANOE GUIDES
Canoeist's Guide to the North-East
LAKE DISTRICT AND MORECAMBE BAY
Coniston Copper Mines
Scrambles in the Lake District (North)
Scrambles in the Lake District (South)
Walks in Silverdale and Arnside AONB
Short Walks in Lakeland 1 – South
Short Walks in Lakeland 2 – North
Short Walks in Lakeland 3 – West
The Tarns of Lakeland Vol 1 – West
The Tarns of Lakeland Vol 2 – East
The Cumbria Way & Allerdale Ramble
Lake District Winter Climbs
Roads and Tracks of the Lake District
The Lake District Angler's Guide
Rocky Rambler's Wild Walks
An Atlas of the English Lakes
Tour of the Lake District
The Cumbria Coastal Way
NORTH-WEST ENGLAND
Walker's Guide to the Lancaster Canal
Family Walks in the Forest Of Bowland
Walks in Ribble Country

Historic Walks in Cheshire
Walking in Lancashire
Walks in Lancashire Witch Country
The Ribble Way
THE ISLE OF MAN
Walking on the Isle of Man
The Isle of Man Coastal Path
PENNINES AND NORTH-EAST ENGLAND
Walks in the Yorkshire Dales
Walks on the North York Moors, books 1 and 2
Walking in the South Pennines
Walking in the North Pennines
Walking in the Wolds
Waterfall Walks – Teesdale and High Pennines
Walking in County Durham
Yorkshire Dales Angler's Guide
Walks in Dales Country
Historic Walks in North Yorkshire
South Pennine Walks
Walking in Northumberland
Cleveland Way and Yorkshire Wolds Way
The North York Moors
DERBYSHIRE, PEAK DISTRICT, EAST MIDLANDS
High Peak Walks
White Peak Walks Northern Dales
White Peak Walks Southern Dales
Star Family Walks Peak District & South Yorkshire
Walking In Peakland
Historic Walks in Derbyshire
WALES AND WELSH BORDERS
Ascent of Snowdon
Welsh Winter Climbs
Hillwalking in Wales – Vol 1
Hillwalking in Wales – Vol 2
Scrambles in Snowdonia
Hillwalking in Snowdonia
The Ridges of Snowdonia
Hereford & the Wye Valley
Walking Offa's Dyke Path
Lleyn Peninsula Coastal Path
Anglesey Coast Walks
The Shropshire Way
Spirit Paths of Wales
Glyndwr's Way
The Pembrokeshire Coastal Path
Walking in Pembrokeshire
The Shropshire Hills – A Walker's Guide
MIDLANDS
The Cotswold Way
The Grand Union Canal Walk
Walking in Warwickshire
Walking in Worcestershire
Walking in Staffordshire
Heart of England Walks

SOUTHERN ENGLAND
Exmoor & the Quantocks
Walking in the Chilterns
Walking in Kent
Two Moors Way
Walking in Dorset
A Walker's Guide to the Isle of Wight
Walking in Somerset
The Thames Path
Channel Island Walks
Walking in Buckinghamshire
The Isles of Scilly
Walking in Hampshire
Walking in Bedfordshire
The Lea Valley Walk
Walking in Berkshire
The Definitive Guide to Walking in London
The Greater Ridgeway
Walking on Dartmoor
The South West Coast Path
Walking in Sussex
The North Downs Way
The South Downs Way
SCOTLAND
Scottish Glens 1 – Cairngorm Glens
Scottish Glens 2 – Atholl Glens
Scottish Glens 3 – Glens of Rannoch
Scottish Glens 4 – Glens of Trossach
Scottish Glens 5 – Glens of Argyll
Scottish Glens 6 – The Great Glen
Scottish Glens 7 – The Angus Glens
Scottish Glens 8 – Knoydart to Morvern
Scottish Glens 9 – The Glens of Ross-shire
The Island of Rhum
Torridon – A Walker's Guide
Walking the Galloway Hills
Border Pubs & Inns – A Walkers' Guide
Scrambles in Lochaber
Walking in the Hebrides
Central Highlands: 6 Long Distance Walks
Walking in the Isle of Arran
Walking in the Lowther Hills
North to the Cape
The Border Country – A Walker's Guide
Winter Climbs – Cairngorms
The Speyside Way
Winter Climbs – Ben Nevis & Glencoe
The Isle of Skye, A Walker's Guide
The West Highland Way
Scotland's Far North
Walking the Munros Vol 1 – Southern, Central
Walking the Munros Vol 2 – Northern & Cairngorms